LIVING BET

Living Between Worlds

PLACE AND JOURNEY IN CELTIC SPIRITUALITY

PHILIP SHELDRAKE

DARTON·LONGMAN+TODD

First published in 1995 by
Darton, Longman and Todd Ltd
1 Spencer Court
140–142 Wandsworth High Street
London SW18 4JJ

ISBN 0–232–52119–0

A catalogue record for this book is available from the British Library

Acknowledgements

Extracts from *A Celtic Miscellany* by Kenneth Hurlstone Jackson, first
published by Routledge & Kegan Paul, are reproduced by permission.

Extracts from *Carmina Gadelica* are reproduced by permission of the Scottish
Academic Press.

Cover: The Lichfield Gospels (720–730 AD), *The Carpet Page*, courtesy of
Sonia Halliday Photographs. Design by Bet Ayer.

Phototypeset by Intype, London
Printed and bound in Great Britain by
Page Bros, Norwich

Contents

Preface

In a rather remote sense, this book has its origins in aspects of my family history and childhood experiences. Although my surname is unmistakably Anglo-Saxon, I am able to appeal to distant (and very diluted) Celtic ancestry on both sides of my family – Irish, Welsh and Scottish. However, my sense of connection with the Celtic world has more to do with landscape than with genes. I was born and brought up in a part of southern England (now in Dorset) with an ancient landscape full of Celtic sites and other echoes. These fascinated me from an early age. Many of my childhood summer holidays were spent with relatives in the north of Yorkshire with regular visits to the Whitby of St Hilda and the Northumberland of St Cuthbert.

More directly, the book took shape during a sabbatical in 1992. I worked on a long-term project that focused on the theology and spirituality of place. As a result of a month-long visit to Iona during that time I ended up with far too much Celtic material for a single chapter in a book on 'place'. Thus, the idea of a distinct book on the Celtic tradition began to grow.

My decision to spend time on Iona owes a great deal to the enthusiasm and persuasiveness of Deborah Douglas in Santa Fe. Sue Daniels, the warden of Duncraig retreat house where I stayed while on the island, created the perfect atmosphere for me to live, walk, meditate and read. I am also grateful to Giles David, then librarian at Iona Abbey, both for enabling me to gain access to the full edition of the *Carmina Gadelica* and other important books and for many stimulating conversations.

Since that time I have had the opportunity to teach about Celtic spirituality and on the history of Celtic Christianity in the Cambridge Theological Federation and at the Summer Institute of Retreats International at the University of Notre Dame. The reactions of students have been very helpful. I acknowledge a scholarly limitation in that I read Latin but no Celtic language.

vii

However, many of the important early texts are in Latin. I have also had useful conversations with people who do understand one or other of the Celtic languages.

I am especially grateful to my colleague Dr David Cornick of Westminster College for continuing conversations about Celtic Christian history, for drawing my attention to complex questions of interpretation and for reading a draft of this book. Sister Catherine Thom, who lectures at the Catholic University of Australia, also commented helpfully on the draft. Of course, I take full responsibility for any errors and for the particular interpretations I have adopted. Finally, thanks are due to Morag Reeve at Darton, Longman and Todd for her interest in and support for the project.

Philip Sheldrake
Cambridge, 1995

Place and Journey

It is important to be clear at the outset what this book is and is not. First of all, it is a book about *spirituality* – specifically the spiritual traditions that grew up among the Celtic peoples of the British Isles. My purpose is not to provide a comprehensive historical introduction to Celtic Christianity as a whole. It is true that there is an urgent need for such an overall introduction. For one thing there has been a great increase of interest in Celtic matters over the last few years. Celtic Christianity is becoming something of an industry. Talks and courses now abound and popular books are beginning to proliferate.

A great deal has also happened in the scholarly world, thanks to the writings of people such as Nora Chadwick, Kathleen Hughes, Charles Thomas and some revisionist historians. Sadly the gap between their work and popular writing is often substantial. The absence of a reliable and up-to-date general history of Celtic Christianity that bridges the gap between modern scholarship and the general interest on both sides of the Atlantic is a serious one.

My aim in this book is in a modest way to help to bridge that gap but within a very specific focus. Even 'spirituality' is a fairly broad topic and this book does not pretend to do full justice to every aspect of it in relation to Celtic Christianity. I have instead used a particular framework of interpretation which I hope will enable us to look at the topic of 'Celtic spirituality' in a fresh way. The dialectic between an attachment to 'place' and a desire for 'the journey' among early Celtic Christians provides a particularly interesting key to our understanding of this tradition.

'Celtic spirituality' is itself an ambiguous phrase. The enthusiasm of contemporary 'rediscovery' must not lead us to forget that Celtic people, experiencing Christian faith within Celtic cultural contexts, exist in a continuous line up to the present

1

day. In that sense 'Celtic Christianity' never died out. What did happen was that after the twelfth century (and much earlier in some places) the distinctive approach to Christian life-style, law and liturgy effectively ceased to exist in Celtic areas. Celtic Christians simply became one other racial grouping within an increasingly homogenous western, Latin Christendom. What survived as distinctive tended to be the more popular devotional aspects of religion. The power of these should not be underestimated (as evidenced by the material gathered by Carmichael in Scotland as late as the nineteenth century). However, my main concentration in this book is on the period before the twelfth century when the Celtic version of Christianity had distinctive structural and public forms.

How are we to explain the present fascination with Celtic Christianity and spirituality in particular? The reasons for the renaissance are perhaps not hard to find. In general terms the last thirty years have seen a strong reassertion of regional identity in the British Isles. This movement has been predominantly Celtic. While this does not have a direct bearing on spirituality it has an indirect one. This is because Celtic culture in its varied forms has become more widely known and appreciated than it was before the 1960s.

There are also a number of factors that are specifically religious. In the English-speaking (and, indeed, Gaelic-speaking) world there is a serious dissatisfaction with the institutional Church. This is leading an increasing number of people to seek in the past a version of Christianity that seems to be free from all that they find unattractive about the Church's present institutional forms. Such a golden age and such a perfect Christianity never existed, of course, but the temptation to search for it is understandable.

Again, in our post-modern world, there is a cynicism about the claims of the all-embracing systems and traditional structures of Christianity. These, it is felt, no longer provide all that the believer needs and an answer to every eventuality. This attitude affects all of us to differing degrees. In this context, Celtic Christianity is presented as an attractive religious sensibility.

It seems to embrace a more contextual, grounded, varied yet uncomplicated, messy, even chaotic faith and spirituality than the conventional, institutional forms. This appears to be more in tune with the low level of dogmatic certainty and the high level of spiritual desire that characterise Western culture these days. The importance of pilgrimage and journey in the Celtic tradition, balanced with a strong sense of place, are sentiments that are very much in tune with the experience and temper of our own age. We seek both firm roots and yet a capacity to deal with continuous change.

There are other themes that contemporary books on Celtic Christianity so strongly emphasise precisely because they too fit our contemporary needs. Thus, it is said that Celtic Christianity is a religion that is deeply embedded in its surrounding culture and society. It is also full of continuities with its pre-Christian past. The sense that the Celtic form of Christianity has connections with pagan myths and even practices is attractive to people who are influenced by the eclecticism of what are popularly known as 'New Age' movements. Celtic spirituality offers a closeness and sensitivity to the natural world. Last, but not least, the Celtic version of the Church appears to have been less patriarchal than most and to have given leadership roles to women.

It is not that any of these values, themes or analyses of Celtic Christianity are *entirely* false. But the trouble is that too much of the contemporary interest in Celtic religion, and Christianity in particular, is historically simplistic. Consequently, the picture painted is at best one-dimensional and at worst positively misleading. Some popular writing on the subject lacks a real sense of history and the complexity of some of the questions involved.

I believe that the Celtic tradition of Christianity deserves to be retrieved. I have suggested in a previous book that it is an example of a spiritual tradition that did not fit within a Latin Christian hegemony and so was gradually marginalised.[1] However, it also deserves a less romanticised and more balanced treatment. The reality has been obscured by Celtic mists and golden sunsets! In the widespread and traditional view of European culture, the lands of the former Roman Empire continue

3

to mark the bounds of the 'civilised world'. This is a view that many history books have tended to imply even if they do not state it categorically. From this perspective the Celtic lands are geographically off-centre and lie on what is conceived as the far north-west edge of 'the world'. The danger has been that, psychologically too, as writers move into the Celtic mists they fall off the edges of the world of fact into imagination and supposition. Seekers after Celtic remedies for religious and cultural frustration too often manage simply to find an echo of what they so desperately seek.

The common simplification is to give the impression that 'Celtic Christianity' is one-dimensional with no regional variations of any importance. To suggest this, however, would be as crude as to talk of 'the English-speaking world' as though it were a single culture. In fact Celtic religious culture covered, and continues to cover, six different lands grouped into two distinct areas and language groups. The first area consists of Ireland, Scotland and the Isle of Man. The Celtic Church in the North East of England – the former Kingdom of Northumbria – derived from missionaries from this first area. Scottish Gaelic and Manx (now extinct) are really offshoots of Irish. In terms of Christian community life and literature this is the best-documented area and the one on which most books concentrate their attention. The second area, which is also bound together by close cultural and linguistic ties, consists of Wales, Cornwall and Brittany. Breton has been heavily influenced by French but was probably quite close to Cornish originally as a result of emigration from southern Britain in post-Roman times.

Because of the richness of the written sources, most of what has been written about 'Celtic spirituality' has, in practice, been based on Irish forms (including their implantation in Scotland) with a nod in the direction of the Scottish Highland and Hebridean material collected in the nineteenth century by Alexander Carmichael. More recently there have been some attempts to explore specifically Welsh forms of spiritual sensibility.[2] We need to remember, however, that there was a substantial amount of Irish settlement in post-Roman Wales and influence on the

4

development of the Christian Church there even if the Irish language never replaced the local variety.[3] Due care must be exercised in treating material from these distinct areas. However, some degree of generalisation about spiritual values and themes is valid.[4]

Another simplification that very easily becomes complete inaccuracy is to suggest that there was a *totally* separate 'Celtic Church', unconnected to the rest of western Christendom. To speak of 'the Celtic Church', in the sense of an entity that rejected the primacy of Rome, is entirely invalid. There is a myth, that still does the rounds occasionally, that 'the Celtic Church' was some kind of British National Church with doctrines and practices that were uncontaminated by association with the Constantinian corruption of Roman Christianity.

A scattered rural society in Celtic lands, with a long tradition of migration, would naturally think of the Church in a quite different way from the more urbanised and settled world of Roman experience. Thus, a flexible, relatively loose or fluid structure in Celtic Christianity competed with the Roman taste for more structured administration expressed in organised dioceses. Church personnel, such as bishops or priests, became associated less universally than elsewhere with administrative functions. Theirs could be a spiritual ministry that was not necessarily tied to a fixed location. However, despite some cultural differences, the working language of Celtic Christianity was always Latin. Most of the important ecclesiastical texts are in that language.

Our tendency has been to read back into the so-called Dark Ages, or early Middle Ages, a notion of centralised western Catholicism. This only really began to apply, and then to a still limited degree, from the eleventh century onwards. In this anachronistic view, the peculiarities of Celtic Christianity were eccentric to the mainstream. Therefore, it is concluded, it must have been separatist. As a result, some modern historians think that popular phrases like 'the Celtic church' and 'Celtic Christianity' should, given the actual universality of Christianity, be deplored as misleading and inaccurate.[5]

5

There can be no doubt that the Celtic tradition was *distinctive* but this was one legitimate strand among many in a still emerging western Catholic tradition. The latter manifested a much greater degree of cultural, legal and liturgical pluralism than was the case in the High Middle Ages and later. Equally, some popular treatments of key Celtic spiritual values, such as closeness to the natural world, seem to suggest that these were *uniquely* the possession of Celtic Christians. All of these views are unhelpful exaggerations or simplifications.

Celtic Christianity was firmly placed in its surrounding culture. So, following this introductory chapter, I will concern myself briefly in Chapter 1 with some general remarks about how Celtic Christianity was particularly formed by its continuities with what preceded it in time and space. The remainder of the book then moves to consider other aspects of 'place' or 'space' in the Celtic religious mind. Although this will need some qualification later, Celtic Christianity produced a more 'monastic' Church in which episcopacy was not always the dominant organisational system. Religious, political, social and cultural sites tended to blend into each other. How and why particular places in the landscape were chosen for Christian communities is therefore the central question for Chapter 2.

In Chapter 3 I move on to the question of how sacred places were enclosed and divided to designate areas of different significance within them. Because 'religious enclosure' in some form is central to all varieties of religion, 'sacred space' and 'holy places' are vital categories for understanding the Celtic Christian tradition. How was 'enclosure' fixed around and within Celtic communities? What did enclosure signify? Separation from the rest of surrounding culture or a place of inclusion? Protection against the threat of 'outside' or a place of encounter and of an intense concentration of religious experiences? In this context, it is important to note that the texts (often poetry) that emphasise an almost romantic attachment to the solitary life set apart from wider society date from the seventh to the twelfth centuries. This was when the ascetic tradition of exile and 'pilgrimage for Christ' was in decline. Their attitudes cannot therefore be associated unquestioningly with early Celtic Christianity prior to the Synod of Whitby in 664.

Celtic Christians had – and even today, have – a strong sense of living on 'edges' or 'boundary places' between the material world and the other world. The natural landscape was both a concrete reality where people lived and, at the same time, a doorway into another, spiritual, world. Such a notion found a recent powerful voice in the late Dr George MacLeod, the founder of the modern Iona Community and one-time Moderator of the Church of Scotland. He spoke of the Isle of Iona, where St Columba founded his great centre of monasticism and evangelisation, as 'a thin place' where the membrane between this world and the other world, between the material and the spiritual, was very permeable.

This sense of living on boundaries was often marked by the characteristic High Crosses – particularly in Ireland but also present in Scotland and Wales. Boundary places such as crosses, and also places such as cemeteries or shrines, will be the theme of Chapter 4. This sense of living in a 'between place' enabled Celtic Christians to make connections between the physical and the intangible, the seen and the unseen, this world and a permanently present 'other' world.

In contrast to the notion of 'enclosure' and fixed places such as crosses or cemeteries, which speak of stability and of settling in a specific place, Chapter 5 considers the theme of journey, exile and pilgrimage as the central ideal of many Celtic ascetics. As I hope to show, 'journey' can only be fully appreciated in relation to, and in tension with, a strong sense of place, kin and stability. Especially in the later prayers and in the writings of hermits, the sense of place is expressed in a beautiful sense of the natural world as a doorway into the sacred. As Chapter 6 will argue, closeness to nature, and a sense of the sacred in nature, has much to do with an attentiveness to the grounded and embodied quality of religious experience. We need to be aware, however, that most of the texts that appear to romanticise nature in the period from approximately 700 onwards also laud the virtues of a stable, solitary life in contrast to the more unstable

7

and uncouth life-styles of the holy wanderers. They therefore contain elements of propaganda. Equally, the Celtic approach to nature was not unrealistic. Celtic Christians were as aware of its dangerous power and unpredictable quality as they were of its softer hues. They shared, with all their contemporary Europeans, a fear of wilderness, woods and fens. In some respects the Celtic approach to nature was not unique.

'Celtic Christianity' is a multi-faceted reality about which too many generalisations are dangerous. However, it is easiest to note this fact and then to concentrate on one sector, the Irish–Scottish region which not only had intimate interconnections but also was responsible for the Christianisation of what is now North East England. At the heart of this particular Celtic religious 'family' of places lay the island of Iona, St Columba and the monastic community he founded there. My final chapter will look briefly at some of the themes of this book with particular reference to the island and its history of Christian presence.

In Celtic Christian spirituality the values of 'place' and 'journey' are connected closely, albeit paradoxically. This is because both are associated in different ways with the experience of 'transition'. In the full sense implied etymologically by the Latin verb *transire*, 'to go over', journeys between places are self-evidently transitions and movements. But places themselves are not static realities either. All places are transit points, passage-ways between worlds. Both the pilgrimage journey and the sacred place encapsulate a here-and-now experience of *transitus* – the conclusive 'passing over' to the other world that is ultimately brought about by death.

So, an engagement with 'place' (as, for example, in desert monasticism's mystique of 'the cell' or St Benedict's teaching on stability) may enable a spiritual, inner journey. This leads the seeker towards a final dissolution of the boundaries between worlds. Equally, the journey of the wandering ascetics was actually a search for the ultimate *place*, a place of harmony and the unity of all things in the Absolute – what the Celtic ascetics called 'the place of resurrection'.

8

ONE

Continuities in Time and Place

There can be no doubt that Celtic Christians had, and still have, a strongly developed sense of place. Much of this arises from the survival, more than elsewhere in Europe, of a strong sense of extended kin, and of the clan to which one belongs and its traditional centres of habitation. Another important, and related, aspect of Celtic spirituality is the sense of continuity in cultural and religious tradition and in connections with particular landscapes. For example, one of the things that fascinates many modern consumers of Celtic books is the survival of pre-Christian attitudes and practices.

Ancient Survivals

As any student of medieval 'magic' knows, continuities with a pre-Christian past were quite common throughout Europe during the early Middle Ages.[1] However, it is fair to say that the Church in Celtic lands took over wholesale so many of the existing cultural and social structures that it seemed to Christianise traditional religion in a more systematic way. It is also true that the geographical location of the Celtic lands was relatively remote in relation to a 'centre' that was perceived in terms of the See of Rome and the old Roman Empire. This, combined with the exceptionally wild landscape and rural life-style, meant that older practices survived relatively widely even into the modern era.

One example was a ritual, adapted from pre-Christian origins, called the *caim*. This seems to have survived at least into the nineteenth century amongst the people of the Hebridean Islands. In times of danger people would draw a circle around themselves with the index finger of the right hand. They would point and turn round sun-wise, praying to the Trinity to encircle and protect them. As we shall see later, such encircling prayers were quite common in early medieval Celtic monastic or clerical communities.

Traditional sacred times also continued to be observed. *Samain* was the greatest festival of the Celtic year. It was one of the four major turning points of the seasons. It was at the same time the year's end and its beginning at the divide between autumn and winter.[2] *Samain* eventually came to correspond to the Christian Feast Days of All Saints, or All Hallows (1st November), with its Vigil (All Hallows' Eve, 'Hallowe'en') and All Souls (2nd November). The night of All Hallows' Eve, in particular, was the most significant moment. It corresponded to the traditional time when the world of ordinary time and space was thought to be overrun by the forces of magic or the souls of the dead. This was a boundary time when the thin veil between this world and the other world became particularly permeable. Such beliefs blended imperceptibly into the celebrations of the Christian feast.

Origins of Church Organisation

At the heart of the theme of continuities in Celtic religious culture lies the question of where the distinctive pattern of Celtic Christianity came from. As we shall see, there is some evidence that in certain cases even Christian community forms that emerged owed something to pre-Christian traditions such as druidic 'schools' and temple virgins. However, we need to look primarily into the confused world of late Roman Imperial Christianity, especially in those areas that were ethnically Celt, that is the Provinces of Britain and Gaul.

Many modern historians would now argue that Christianity was more widespread in Roman Britain, even before the year 400, than was previously thought.[3] So it seems that, after the collapse of Roman provincial government in the early fifth century, wherever Romanised Britons existed Christian groups among them upheld their religion. An ecclesiastical presence of Romano-British origin is very likely within the relatively large proportion of former Roman Britain that remained largely unaffected by Saxon settlement until about 550. The authentic life

10

of St Patrick indicates that he was from a Romano-British family that produced three generations of Christian officials before and after 400. It seems that the Church in Romano-Celtic Britain was functioning as late as the mid-fifth century in a manner that simply extended its fourth-century role. Certainly, as a general remark, there can be no doubt that in the fifth century Christianity was already firmly established in the British Isles.[4]

From the fifth to the seventh centuries the Church in Britain was mainly a continuation, albeit adapted, of its late Roman predecessor. Yet, we find two ecclesiastical structures that became parallel and interconnected.[5] Firstly, the existence of bishops may be inferred from the known career of St Patrick and from what may be read into comments by Gildas in his often unreliable history of the Celts in the following century. When Augustine was sent with his Roman mission to Kent in 597 both he and the pope, Gregory the Great, were aware that there were bishops already present in Britain. The pope had stated that Augustine's authority was to extend over them but the evidence suggests that the native bishops declined to accept him as primate. Some people have treated this as evidence that the 'Celtic Church' was always autonomous and did not owe allegiance to Rome. In fact, the issue was a more local and human one. Behind the reaction of the British bishops undoubtedly lay a problem of racism born of the hostile relations between Celts and Saxons. The bishops did not wish to be part of an ecclesiastical structure that united the Romano-Celtic and the Saxon-occupied parts of the country. Evidence for the precise role of existing Romano-Celtic bishops and the nature of their dioceses, if such organisation existed, is very slight. In contrast to Irish hagiography, the stories of western British saints (for example, Samson in Cornwall and Dyfrig in Wales) often portray the hero as a bishop. Yet, even in Wales where the emphasis on bishops was stronger than in Ireland we can do no more than guess at the details.[6]

11

Monastic Roots

The second strand in the emerging English Church was peculiarly monastic.[7] Apart from Augustine's Roman mission which consisted of Benedictine monks dispatched by a monastic pope, it was Irish monks who really converted the bulk of the English, not merely in the North East but also in the Midlands and even in parts of the South. Though the Irish accepted the primacy of the Roman See, they tended to keep the local churches which they founded more rooted in a form of monastic organisation than elsewhere. This was a contemporary Irish model. Essentially, the wandering monks founded new 'monastic communities' so evangelisation, if it was a conscious policy, was really the result rather than the cause of monastic settlement. Interestingly, Adomnan in his life of Columba does not make the latter a missionary. It is Bede who gives this impression. Indeed, Bede implies in his *Ecclesiastical History*, inaccurately it seems, that the missionary work of the Iona foundation at Lindisfarne was typical of the Irish Church.[8]

It is worth noting in passing that some modern historians consider that Bede in his *Ecclesiastical History* overestimated the importance of the Synod of Whitby. The Synod took place in 664 CE and settled disputes concerning the dating of Easter and the appropriate style of ecclesiastical tonsure. Many people still believe that the Synod marked a definitive victory of the Church of Rome over the native (that is, Celtic) Church of the British Isles. However, the Synod was actually concerned only with the local Church that was dependent on Lindisfarne. Equally, it dealt only with relatively minor matters rather than with the fundamentals of Church organisation and authority. Bede's interpretation perhaps reflects his personal concern for chronology and therefore about the computation of the date of Easter. At least it seems fair to suggest that Bede's view of Whitby contributed to later, more general, views of the seriousness of the differences between Celtic and Roman ecclesiastical styles. As I have already suggested, the questions at issue were really indicative of the general western Catholic melting pot while the acceptable degree of diversity within it was being explored.

12

As we shall see, a monastic structure eventually achieved a higher profile than conventional episcopal organisation in Ireland for local cultural and social reasons. It is still necessary to ask where the monastic ideas came from. The Irish Christians did not simply invent their style of monasticism from nothing. Where were the continuities?

The answer probably lies in the former Roman Provinces of Gaul and Britain. From the mid-fourth century onwards, the Christians of the increasingly troubled provinces of Gaul and Spain in the declining Roman Empire seem to have explored the monastic ideal, brought from Egypt and Palestine by such figures as John Cassian. In adapting eastern models these ascetics, such as Martin of Tours, established the equivalent of 'deserts' on islands and in forests. These were their natural wilderness landscapes. It seems probable that ascetic enthusiasts visited Roman Britain before the collapse of the Empire. British and Irish Celts, while meeting other monastic examples, were particularly influenced by Martin of Tours. His model seems to have become all-powerful in Britain in the post-Roman period. Martinian monasticism did not produce well-organised communities with a detailed rule, under the strong authority of an abbot. Rather the monasteries were relatively loose gatherings of like-minded people. There was no complex of cloister buildings in the later Benedictine sense, merely an aggregation of buildings grouped fairly haphazardly within a boundary wall. Finally, Martin and his monks were not purely contemplative but engaged in evangelisation.[9] All of these features remained true of Celtic monasticism as it emerged.

There is some archaeological evidence to support a hypothesis that a form of 'monasticism' may have taken root amongst the Christianised villa-owners of western Britain at the end of the fourth century and the beginning of the fifth. Such things had happened in Gaul. If true, this would help to explain how and why there were educated people in fifth-century Britain and Ireland who knew about monastic values. 'Villa-monasteries', or domestic monasticism of some kind, might also have provided a model, adaptable to local Irish circumstances, for some kind of fusion between 'monastic' life and secular communities or social structures.[10] There has been a great deal of romantic attention given to direct connections between Ireland and Egypt. However, the connection with Gaul via late-Roman and post-Roman Britain is likely to have been the main influence on Irish monasticism, although some direct trading links with the eastern Mediterranean cannot be discounted.[11]

As a general conclusion, it seems fair to suggest that monasticism, in the sense of organised communities with fixed rules inhabiting definite sites, only came into being in Celtic Britain from the late fifth century onwards. The degree to which monastic organisation eventually *replaced* earlier territorial bishops seems to have varied. This is true especially of Wales where the inheritance from the Roman Empire was much stronger than in Scotland.

Ireland, of course, had never been part of the Empire and was not influenced by urbanised Roman social organisation.[12] Here, the notion of the kin or *paruchia* ('sphere of influence') of bishop or abbot made far more sense than the geographically defined territory of the 'diocese', derived from late-Roman Imperial administrative models.[13]

Some modern revisionist historians have suggested that bishops did exercise a continued diocesan role in Ireland. Yet, compared to most of the western Church, the social and geographical conditions of Ireland were less favourable to the dominance of a diocesan model of organisation. Again, Bede is partly to blame for giving a misleading impression to many modern historians. He seemed to suggest that the unusual constitution of Iona and its *paruchia* was in fact characteristic of the Celtic Church as a whole.[14]

It is now clear that a purely 'monastic' model for church organisation needs revision. It seems that not only in Wales, but also in Ireland, there was a plurality of organisation: diocesan, monastic and local pastoral units. A rigid antithesis between monastic and conventional pastoral organisation in the Celtic Church is far too crude. It seems likely that diocesan structures did continue to exist but became more 'invisible' in comparison

14

to the dominance of monastic terminology in church organisation and to the system of great monastic *paruchia*.[15]

There have been some interesting speculations on the decline
of an episcopal church in the Celtic areas.[16] Normal diocesan
organisation was based on the existence of significant locations
called 'towns' with the metropolitan authority of archbishops
present in regional capitals. This social infrastructure survived
in Britain only as long as Roman organisation did. As the towns
withered, so such a system decayed. The Romanised Celtic *duces*
turned their military commands into independent princedoms.
These were gradually divided into still smaller units. Each
'prince' sought his own bishop. Diocesan boundaries changed
with every political change. There was an increasing mismatch
between the system and the Church's needs and the more flexible
monastic *paruchia* seemed a satisfactory solution.

While it is possible that Patrick initially organised the Church
in parts of Ireland into an episcopal form modelled on the British
Church, the subject is controversial and the evidence slight.[17]
The Romanised Britons gradually reverted to older tribal, kinship alliances. In Ireland such a system was never superseded in
the first place. So during the sixth and seventh centuries, the
dioceses receded while federations of religious communities
became more prominent – each with its wider family, or *paruchia*, under the supreme jurisdiction of the *conarb* or heir of the
founder saint. The non-territorial allegiances allowed the 'local'
Church to expand indefinitely as its followers travelled widely.
Pastoral and spiritual authority lay less with institutional structures, as in episcopal government, and more with personal spiritual advisors – the *anamchara* in Ireland and the *periglour* in
Wales.[18] Bishops ceased to relate exclusively to structures of
Church discipline or to geographical units. Their numbers actually grew. Legend has it that when Columba sailed to Iona he
took no less than twenty bishops with him![19]

The Celtic Church developed a different sense of religious
'location' from the Roman concept of anchoring spiritual
authority to cities of great antiquity. These different concepts of
'location' really masked different understandings of 'being a

local Church' and how the local should function in relation to the universal. This is a much more significant and valid contrast than the supposed doctrinal divisions between Celtic and Roman Christianity that were once suggested by earlier commentators.[20]

It seems probable that in Ireland a much larger proportion of the population than anywhere else in the Celtic world (or indeed western Catholicism in general) lived within what might be called 'monastic' space. Nowhere else was the culture of a whole people so completely embraced within quasi-monastic structures and a monastic terminology. Historians have adduced very different reasons for this. Some suggest that Irish religious culture, from pre-Christian times, was peculiarly susceptible to ascetic urges. It has also been said that the tremendous talent and energy to be found in traditional Irish art and the great druidic tradition of learning found safeguards for their survival in monastic structures.[21]

Both of these suggestions may be true. But other historians have provocatively suggested that we beg the question by calling the Celtic forms of Christian community by the term 'monastic'.[22] The peculiar fusion of religious and social structures means that we cannot speak of an overall monastic 'vocation' in a proper sense. What I mean is that we would normally be looking for reasons why so many people *entered* monasteries. However, especially in Ireland, what we have, as we shall see later, is the monasticising of local settlements. 'The monastery' and its extended family of settlements, or *paruchia*, was the essential model for the local Church. So, at the early stage of the shift from a more episcopal to a more monastic Church structure it is difficult to speak of 'monasteries' as intentional or voluntary communities in the normal sense. Socially speaking, you could be born into a local 'monastery' settlement and religiously speaking you were baptised into a version of the local Church. Gradually, from within these local Churches emerged specific and voluntary ascetical life-styles, whether solitary or communitarian such as the so-called Culdees or *celi de*. We also need to bear in mind that Celtic and Anglo-Saxon areas seem to have shared a common tendency to use monastic terminology even for secular clergy gathered around a 'minster' or large regional church.

It is interesting that some continuities between religious organisation and Irish social attitudes and structures managed to survive, at least for a time, the twelfth-century ecclesiastical reforms which came with Norman influence and occupation. The reforms demanded the separation of the laity from ecclesiastical professionals whether the latter were clergy or monastic ascetics. While the elaborate liturgical and cenobitic life of traditional Benedictine monasteries did not take root in Ireland, the new orders of Cistercians and Augustinian canons and canonesses flourished. It is possible that the popularity of Cistercian asceticism or Augustinian flexibility and evangelising spirit rather than Benedictine monasticism reflects continuities with Celtic spiritual values and traditions. There were continuities of place as well. It is estimated that about half of the 'new' Augustinian communities of canons and canonesses in Ireland from the twelfth century were on the sites of earlier monasteries. Indeed, some of the older Celtic communities may simply have adopted the Augustinian Rule.[23]

Despite these changes, monks and laity continued to a large extent to live in close proximity as they had for centuries. Even the austere and supposedly enclosed Cistercians developed relations of interaction with nearby settlements. The order recruited so many Irish people (or perhaps absorbed already existing ascetic groups) that it quickly went native. Irish abbots, once elected, returned to traditionally independent ways and refused to attend the annual general chapter at Citeaux! The formal, rectangular stone cloisters of Benedictine–Cistercian monasticism were unpopular from the start. It is recorded that when St Malachy tried to persuade the monks of Armagh to build a rectangular cloister, they replied *Scotti sumus non galli* – 'We're Irish, not Gauls!'. When a Cistercian Abbot Visitor came to Ireland in the mid-thirteenth century he found that the monks had returned to living in traditional wattle huts outside the stone cloisters that they had been forced to build to satisfy the regulations of their order.[24]

17

During the earlier advance of Benedictine monasticism into formerly Celtic Northumbria many older features were retained. In Bede's time, the monasteries at Monkwearmouth and Jarrow retained the Celtic tradition of individual cells, at least for older monks, and a pattern of varied buildings within a *cashel* or *vallum*.[25]

Continuities of Place

I have already mentioned that kinship and place played an important role in Celtic culture. Continuities in Celtic religious experience were closely associated with place because of the Celtic tendency to name places in terms of event. Christian places in the landscape also show this continuity of association. This was the case partly because the original Celtic church sites were simply planted on pre-Christian places of religious or social significance. For example, Armagh in Ireland takes its name (*Ard Macha*) from a pagan goddess.[26]

In a pre-Christian Celtic religious context, the most widespread form of sacred space would have been a wood or a tract of ground on which stood a grove of trees. Next in order of importance came the places at which seasonal gatherings of the tribe took place. Thus there were various rural sacred sites in Ireland (for example, Emain Macha, Tara, Cruachain, Knockaulin) that had particular associations with tribal celebrations, races and games. Often the important sites were linked to grave mounds, though not all Celtic sanctuaries were places of burial. It is worth recalling here the traditional link between early Christian sacred sites and the graves of saints.[27] Later Irish monasteries were often founded as guardians of shrines of saints which became the centre of an ongoing tradition of worship and pilgrimage.[28]

England has a small quota of parish churches that overlie sites of pre-Christian Romano-Celtic temples.[29] It is difficult to know whether such sites retained a specifically religious significance at the time when Christian churches were founded. Connections between later church sites and earlier sacred wells seem to be far more common. The large number of church dedications to St Helen may in fact refer to Ellen, the Celtic goddess of three heads who is associated with wells.[30] Even today, in the Celtic parts of the British Isles, wells are still remembered as places of healing, fertility or good luck. Some of them have explicitly Christian associations, such as the relatively important pilgrimage shrine to St Winifred at Holywell in North Wales. Other insignificant rural wells, even in Presbyterian Scotland, still attract locals today in ways that are scarcely Christianised at all.

Pagan deities were sometimes retained in Christian demonology but not all of them were down-graded like this. It has been suggested that in the evangelisation of Roman Gaul there was a wholesale Christian substitution for sites associated with the god Mercury.[31] The attributes and even names of earlier gods were, as we have seen already, kept alive by the early Irish Church and allocated to saints. There was often a striking fusion of symbolisms. This went further than a mere superimposition of Christian symbols on pre-Christian forms as happened more widely during the conversion of Europe.[32]

A good example would be Kildare where the stories of the abbess St Brigit took over from the goddess of the same name, alternatively called Brig or Bride. There, the temple of the fertility goddess had nine virgin priestesses who tended an eternal fire.[33] It seems that the Christian abbess and nuns simply assumed some at least of the traditional religious duties even to the extent that the fire continued to burn. Kildare also provides evidence of the way some monastic sites were connected with ancient sacred trees for the name of the monastery of St Brigit comes from *Cell Dara*, 'the church of the oak wood'.[34] In general, however, connections between pre-Christian gods and Christians saints were more complex than simple one-to-one substitutions.

The example of Kildare reminds us that continuities existed not only in terms of gods and sacred places but also in terms of sacred personnel. The most obvious case would be that of the druids. As we shall see later, large monastic settlements continued the druidic and bardic tradition of centres of learning and education. In the light of modern studies in comparative religion, druids were part of a well-defined socio-religious category common to many Indo-European societies. However, the druids were not a hereditary clan or caste, unlike the Brahmins of India for example. They were recruited from within a warrior aristocracy and in this show similarities with later Celtic Christian ascetics. The word 'druid' may relate to 'knowledge of the oak' (the oak being especially associated with the divine) or even 'deep knowledge'. Without claiming more than can be proved, this role of mediating divine knowledge accords well with the later role of the Celtic ascetics and 'soul friends'.[35]

The pantheon of old gods could be translated fairly easily into the Christian belief in angels. So the old gods could survive as a lower grade of spiritual beings under a single, supreme God. On occasion, the evangelisation process in the Saxon world, both in Germany under St Boniface and in England, seems to have involved such a process of translation. St Michael the Archangel (often linked with dedications to 'All Angels') was particularly popular for parish churches in England and Wales. Before the era of Victorian expansion in church-building, roughly 6 per cent of all churches were dedicated to St Michael.

The dioceses of Hereford and Exeter were both, significantly, in areas with traditions of Celtic cultural survival. There, St Michael was near the top of the league table of church dedications. Interestingly, early medieval Christians seem to have felt that Michael and angels would be particularly at home on hilltops. We only have to think of the chapel on the top of Glastonbury Tor and the islands with high rocky pinnacles such as Skellig Michael off County Kerry, Mont St Michel off the coast of Normandy and St Michael's Mount off Cornwall. The continuity of association with pre-Christian 'high places' seems obvious. Mont St Michel, for example, was built following a supposed vision of the archangel on what was actually a traditional wooded Celtic burial mound!

In general, it seems fair to say that the greatest spiritual continuity was in overall perceptions of the spiritual power associated with traditional Celtic cultural and religious sites.

There was a basic cosmology, or sense of how the universe was constructed, that lay behind pre-Christian religion. This was to some degree carried forward into the Christian period. The Irish Celts, for example, felt themselves to be surrounded by gods who were close at hand rather than distant and disengaged. These gods protected the people and their divine spouses ensured fertility and protected the earth from hostile powers. Between the gods and the people were the heroes from whom the princely families of the clans were descended. The clan chief was therefore deemed to be responsible for the material welfare of the people and for balancing the cosmic forces that surrounded everyone and influenced their lives. At the time of their enthronement rites, the clan chief and his wife were invested with magical power.[36] Both places and people effectively preserved this inheritance in a new version of the old sacred universe now framed within Christian community structures. So the sacred place of the 'monastery' took on the aspect of the clan enclosure and the abbot or abbess replaced the sacred ruler, or sometimes combined both roles.

Because 'place' was so central to the Celtic religious and cultural mentality, an exploration of the reasoning that lies behind the chosen locations of Christian religious sites is an interesting subject. Clearly, continuity with traditional cultural or religious centres was a frequent factor. However, there was a fascinating variety of both practical and symbolic reasons for choosing particular geographical sites. It is to this question that I now wish to turn my attention.

TWO

Landscape and Sacred Sites

There are two aspects of the Celtic Christian tradition that seem to be generally well known. First, the Church was unusually influenced by monasticism. Second, the Celtic form of monasticism was characterised by a strong ascetical tendency and by the existence of numerous hermits living in wild and isolated places. However, the significance of both of these elements is a matter of quite subtle interpretation. The 'desert' or wilderness in its various forms has exercised a peculiar fascination for spiritual seekers throughout Christian history. This is especially true of the originators of what we call the 'monastic movement' in Syria, Palestine and Egypt in the fourth century.

> Christian monasticism . . . originated in the kingdom of the scorpion and the hyena: a world of rock and heat. Several centuries later the biographers of holy men in north-west Europe depicted their subjects as seekers after landscapes and environments which were correspondingly forbidding.[1]

There have been plenty of attempts to describe a special connection between religious experience and 'the desert', however the latter is understood.[2] Even in the west, this connection is not unique to Celtic Christianity. The history of the western Church throughout the Middle Ages is full of anchorites who fled into the wilderness – that is to say, to islands or to forests. The theme of the 'desert' is common to many monastic and hermit texts. It is both a paradise, where people may live in harmony with wild animals, and at the same time a place of trial where ascetics encounter the inner and outer demons.

Deserts: Seclusion or Access?
It is interesting to note that in the Celtic lands quite a number of traditional Christian sites are commemorated in modern place names by the various local words for 'desert'. Thus in Scotland

it is Dysart, in Wales it is Dysserth or Dyserth and it is Diseart in Ireland. In the Hebrew scriptures there are close ties between the wilderness, the ocean, and the themes of death and the other world. These same themes and connections are apparent in the Celtic tradition as well. While earlier traditions probably played a part, it may be that the Celtic ascetics who went to sea in search of 'the desert' had also been encouraged by their regular monastic reading of the Old Testament. Adomnan's *Life of Columba* speaks of the monks who 'have recently gone out desiring to find a desert place in the sea that cannot be crossed'.[3]

The great Celtic saints such as Columba of Iona and Cuthbert of Lindisfarne seemed to find their special 'deserts' on the borderlands of normal settlement patterns. The British Isles are full of caves, Roman ruins, islands and coastal headlands with Celtic Christian associations and remains. Indeed, almost all the islands around the coast of Britain have remains of chapels dedicated to Celtic saints.[4]

The Irish medieval 'penitentials', or handbooks for priests concerning confession, indicate that spiritual values and social expectations were in a constant state of tension in the development of Christian community. The uneasy reciprocity between these values was reflected in the wide range of sites chosen by Celtic ascetics for their life-style. Some sites were obviously marginal places shunned by ordinary people. Other sites were comfortable and attractive places with access to natural and human resources. Indeed, they were often already social centres of some significance. Recent scholarship has emphasised how the choice of religious sites took account of both spiritual and practical factors. Many notable sites were close to good natural resources such as water. Others were deliberately associated with traditional holy places. In both cases, therefore, these sites were places where ordinary people tended to live already or where they regularly gathered for cultural, political and religious purposes.[5]

A wealth of archaeological evidence suggests that the most favoured natural sites for religious settlement were those that offered a combination of seclusion and access.[6] While the writers of Celtic saints' lives frequently praised their heroes for fleeing human society, the reality of saintly lives was more ambiguous. If we look at the geographical spread of monastic communities we see that the ascetical deserts, especially in Ireland, were rarely far away from settlement clusters or ring forts. In Wales, it has been suggested that many Celtic churches were placed near what were called bond-vills, that is to say, nucleated settlements of serfs around the residence of a local lord. This development took place in the immediate post-Roman period. So large numbers of what are today isolated church sites are the result of the decline in bond-vills by the time of Anglo-Norman settlement rather than of a deliberate option for isolation.[7]

Even the biographies of Celtic saints gave mixed reviews to the extreme solitaries. The story of the Irish St Mochuda records that he denounced St Cronan for his supposedly inconsiderate behaviour because the latter had withdrawn to a remote hermitage. 'To a man who avoids guests and builds his church in a wild bog, away from a level road, I will not go.' On the other hand, a life of St Cronan himself suggests a different story but similar values. Here Cronan moved his monastery because people failed to find him. 'I will not be in a desert place where guests and poor people cannot easily find me, but I will stay here in a public place.' Apparently he then settled at Roscrea where today there is a Cistercian monastery.[8]

Yet, to the modern eye, many of the sites we know about still appear to be very remote and wild. For example, there were the many island sites. Caldey Island off the coast of South Wales, where there is a modern monastic foundation, was popular with individual hermits or small groups of ascetics. Off the coast of Brittany, the small archipelago of Bréhat in the Gulf of St Malo had monastic settlements on a number of islands. Ile Lavré, dedicated to St Bredoc, had a monastery built in the ruins of a Roman villa. Its plan closely resembled fourth- or fifth-century Syrian monastic *lauras* and indeed it has been argued that the island's name is derived from the Syriac word. This, if accurate, would reinforce the belief of some historians that there were close connections between Celtic and eastern Mediterranean monasticism.[9]

We need to remember, however, that the Celtic lands often had inhospitable landscapes and few trackways. For this reason, the sea was a means of connection and communication as well as a cause of separation. This may explain the popularity of those islands, such as Lindisfarne off the Northumbrian coast or Mont St Michel in northern France, that were cut off at high tide but otherwise attached to the mainland. Peninsulas and headlands offered the same mixture of seclusion and accessibility as the tidal islands. A number of seventh-century monastic settlements along the coast of Northumberland in North East England, such as St Abb's Head, Hartlepool, Tynemouth and Whitby, followed such a pattern of favouring headland sites.

Undoubtedly, religious sites such as Iona, Lindisfarne and Bradwell-juxta-Mare (on the coast of present-day Essex) were wild places, battered by strong winds and thundering seas. The more ascetic Celtic monastics seem not to have feared the wildness of sea nor quailed before lashing rain, gales or bitter cold. However, from the available evidence, it would be false to suggest that either remoteness or discomfort were the sole or universal motivations for Celtic religious settlement. Nor is it the case that the more inhospitable the site the more virtuous the community or individual ascetic! For example, although Bede may have been a biased witness, he wrote with disapproval of St Abb's Head. In doing so, he quoted the criticisms of the Irish monk Adamnan concerning the feasting, gossiping and wearing of rich and elaborate garments.[10]

Hills and Forts

Not all Celtic ascetics settled near the sea. Inland hilltops were also favoured sites. Malmesbury in Wiltshire, later a wealthy Benedictine Abbey, seems to have taken its name from a seventh-century Irish hermit Mailduibh who lived on top of the nearby hill. The visually extraordinary Glastonbury Tor, which rises sharply out of the surrounding Somerset plain, appears to have been occupied by a British monastic settlement in the sixth

25

century. Hilltops, rather like headlands or tidal islands, had a dual purpose. In this case they were both naturally isolated yet conspicuous. Their purpose may not have been so different from the pillars of Syrian ascetics such as Simon Stylites. In addition, of course, hills and high places featured prominently in the Hebrew and Christian scriptures as religious sites or focuses for mystical encounters with the divine. This may have appealed to the biblically-minded Celts.

The practical problem with settlements on hills is that they tend to lack convenient water sources. While this may have attracted the more hard-bitten ascetics, it was actually more common for Celtic monastic settlements to be founded on level ground overlooking running water. In Ireland, the foundation of the monastery of Maedoc at Ros Imber was linked to a legend concerning the place where angels sang. But Ros Imber was also the spot where a lough met two rivers. This provided a ready means of access as well as a plentiful supply of water and fish. Monastic settlements by springs or wells may have continued ancient traditions of holy places. However, the reason why such water sources were thought of as holy in the first place may be inextricably linked to the practical necessities of drinking, cleansing and healing.[11]

While Ireland had never been occupied by the Romans, and Scotland only intermittently so, old forts and walled towns provided Celtic monks with shelter all over the former Roman Province of Britain. This was particularly the case with the system of nine stone forts, the so-called 'Saxon Shore', that stretched around the South East coast from Norfolk to Hampshire. So, for example, St Cedd built his (still surviving) church at Bradwell in Essex from the stones of the former Roman fort of Othona. St Fursa occupied Burgh Castle. At Reculver in Kent there was a church dating from 669. At Richborough, also in Kent and the most important Roman monument in Britain, there are the remains of chapel foundations. What seems to have attracted Celtic ascetics to the former territory of the Roman military commander known as 'The Count of the Saxon Shore' was once again a combination of relative isolation from the land and yet ease of access and movement by sea.

So there can be no doubt that it was the ascetical aspirations of the Celts that attracted them to many of the places that we know were religious settlements, whatever social or economic reasons may also have come into play. The island of Inner Farne drew Cuthbert into greater solitude from Lindisfarne partly because it had the daunting reputation that no one could stay there long because of the attacks of demons. Cedd probably chose as his home what is now the village of Lastingham on the edge of the North York Moors because the bleak landscape was daunting in itself and, according to Bede, was remote and more suited to robbers.

> Cedd chose a site for the monastery among the high and remote hills, which seemed more suitable for the dens of robbers and haunts of wild beasts than for human habitation. His purpose in this was to fulfil the prophecy of Isaiah: 'in the habitation of dragons, where each lay, shall be grass, with reeds and rushes', so that the fruits of good works might spring up where formerly lived only wild beasts, or men who lived like wild beasts.[12]

It was the isolated, remote settlements (or those that eventually became such) that have often survived best. This is because they were not plundered for their stone. Ireland is particularly well-equipped with ancient sites because the landscape has not been overtaken by a major industrial revolution. In contrast, many English sites are now surrounded by towns and industrial, or former industrial, sites. Bede's Jarrow, for example, lies on the outskirts of a large industrialised town. This contrasts sharply with the empty bays and windswept headlands of rural Ireland. As Kathleen Hughes, one of the leading modern historians of the Irish Church, has noted,

> A hundred yards outside the monastic enclosure the physical experience is the same for us as for them: 'A clear-voiced cuckoo sings to me', the sound of the 'white-waved sea' is unchanged.[13]

One of the most dramatic and remote examples of a surviving

Irish site is Skellig Michael, 8 miles off County Kerry. Here a rock, 2000 feet from end to end and 715 feet high, rises abruptly out of the sea. The monastic site was more or less at the top. The settlement was contemplative yet consisted not of a single hermit's cell but of a community of six people with two chapels, a cemetery and a garden.[14] Inishmurray, off the coast of Sligo, also appears remote but its unusually large stone enclosing wall, *cashel*, may mean that it took over from a prince's fort.[15]

Settlements and Travel

The idealisation of remoteness expresses only one aspect of Celtic, and especially Irish, religious settlement. Nearly all the major sites that grew into important monasteries are in fact on major travel routes or at least, in terms of ancient human geography, in relatively accessible places. The setting of the monastic settlement on the island of Nendrum or Mahee on the western shores of Strangford Lough in Northern Ireland is interesting. The site is on the *landward* side of the island, facing the mainland. So it seems that the founder, St Mochaoi, who had arrived by sea, chose a site where there was a territory to evangelise in front while behind was the sea lough with its potential for contact with the outside world. There was in fact an important gateway in the outer earthwork complete with janitor's cell that led to a quayside. This emphasises the supreme importance of sea communications to such sites. The site utilised an old ring fort though it does not seem that it was still occupied in a military or civil way.[16]

The windy and rainy environment of Ireland provided only a limited range of choices for safe and comfortable settlements. For example, hills stood comfortably apart from the soft, boggy soil of the valleys which made cross-country travel so difficult. It is not surprising that some of these dry 'islands' also boasted secular forts: for example, Armagh and Cashel. Estuaries, lake-sides and coastline were the natural communications routes for a land that was largely without roads. This no doubt explains the settlements on Strangford Lough and on the Isle of Iona which conveniently straddled the sea route from Ulster to Scotland.[17]

It is an interesting question as to how far the pattern of religious sites in Ireland reflects traditional Irish settlements and how far the imported ideals of desert monasticism. In the end, it is difficult to distinguish the two. This is because spiritual ideals were so effectively inculturated into the social fabric and embedded into the realities and limitations of the landscape. The archaeology of the Irish Church tends to suggest that traditional building structures and social forms were frequently adapted to church use. This means that even after careful excavation it is not always possible to tell the difference between a secular site and a religious one. Often the only distinguishing features would be the presence of religious artwork or evidence from burials.

The typical religious settlement seems to have been enclosed within a *vallum*, or bank of earth (as at Iona) or of stone, that often resembled an ordinary ring fort. Indeed, there are several examples of sites where an actual fort was reused for religious purposes or where monastery and royal fort co-existed in the same general enclosure. In early Christian Ireland, monasteries were the only truly nucleated settlements. Although they were sometimes referred to as 'cities' they also contained specialised religious communities and centres of learning. The settlement at Clonard, for example, seems to have accommodated more than a thousand people.[18]

Boundary Places

It has been suggested by some recent scholars that monastic settlements were often deliberately sited on the boundaries between kingdoms.[19] The motivation for this seems to have been complex. Some of the reasons were quite practical and tend to reinforce a sense that religious groups and their sites were closely associated with secular society rather than rigidly separated from it. Thus, boundary lands had traditionally been seen as suitable places for royal forts. Public events such as fairs were held there. It is also likely that the boundaries between territories marked the lines of the few routes that ran across the landscape.

Moreover, it seems that the boundaries of kingdoms were sometimes occupied by ritual sites used for assemblies or more general pre-Christian religious activities. Monastic settlements in these places were in some sense in continuity with this religious tradition. However, the issue is deeper than this. The Celts also had a fascination for the spiritual quality of boundary places. Living on physical boundaries also symbolised a state of liminality – of living literally and spiritually on the margins or between two worlds, the material one and the spiritual one. We have already seen that Lastingham in Yorkshire, like so many Celtic sites, was frontier territory. Lastingham was on the border between the rich agricultural settlements of the Vale of Pickering and the wilderness of the high moors. Boundaries and frontiers of a physical kind were among the places where Celts experienced the veil that separated this world and the other world to be particularly transparent.

Sacred Landscapes

So, in choosing sites for religious settlements different spiritual and practical factors were taken into consideration. Place had a sacred significance. The Christian Celts were as concerned as their ancestors had been about the issue of the sacred landscape and about good or evil places. They accepted that two worlds came together at certain familiar places in the landscape. Christian ascetics therefore sought out places where, in some special way, heaven appeared to meet earth. These boundary or frontier places were sometimes associated with traditional sacred places such as woodlands or wells. Some of the great Christian sites retain references to these links in their names. Thus Kildare derives from the words *Cell Dara* or 'the church of the oak wood'. In other places Christian monuments were raised at traditional tribal burial centres. This is because cemeteries, as we shall see, were rather obvious boundary places – doorways from this material world into the spiritual world.

In general, the surviving evidence suggests that Christian religious settlements depended a great deal on the traditional markers in the landscape. This fact was frequently glossed over in specifically Christian stories of origin. Thus, the choice of places was sometimes reinterpreted in hagiographies in terms of saintly or angelic guidance. However, this very method of authenticating choices bears an uncanny resemblance to traditional Celtic approaches to these matters. Here visions of spirits, demons or the gods often played a role!

Spiritually speaking, for Celts not just *any* place in the landscape would do. There was a sense that certain kinds of places had more spiritual potential. This could be because of geography or association. There was another factor that came into play. Individuals and groups of ascetics also seemed to have had a belief that there was *one* precise location in the sacred landscape of the world that was particularly potent for their spiritual destiny. The religious texts associated with the wandering pilgrims, as we shall see in Chapter 5, spoke of them 'seeking the place of their resurrection'. Thus if ascetical wanderers eventually found a place where they chose to settle this was not simply because it was remote, offered material security or even because it was deemed to have some general supernatural significance. It was in a quite specific way discerned to be their particular doorway to heaven.[20]

I hope that I have shown how choices of religious sites reflected certain spiritual values and not merely practical considerations. In summary, three dimensions stand out. First, in the search for holiness and spiritual experience there was a creative tension between the desire for seclusion and the wish to be accessible and open to society at large. This expresses in a particular way a theological balance between transcendence and immanence in the Celtic Christian experience of God. Secondly, there was an unusually symbiotic relationship between the monastic style of Church life and traditional social organisation. This is particularly true of Ireland but, as my comments on late Romano-Celtic Britain show, by no means exclusively so. What we might call monasticism became not merely a specialist way of life for a small number of ascetics but in some form or other *the* way of being Church. Speaking more broadly, spirituality was not something detached from social values and

31

organisation but was intimately entwined with them. This was apparent not least in the extraordinary continuities of ancient holy places in people's consciousness and religious behaviour. Thirdly, there was a fascination with borderlands and liminality particularly associated with a strong sense of the closeness of the 'other' world to the world of everyday experience. To an extent, all places were points of access, or doorways to the sacred. But certain places or points were marked off as special or particular, for example, cemeteries, monastic enclosures or certain natural features with a long spiritual history.

THREE

Enclosing Sacred Spaces

When we reflect on the nature of Celtic religious settlements, it is not merely their sites that had spiritual significance. The ways in which such settlements were marked out in the landscape by various kinds of boundaries, as well as the ways in which they were internally ordered, also reveal important aspects of Celtic spiritual attitudes.

The hagiographies of Celtic saints, such as Adomnan's life of Columba, are fanciful by modern biographical and historical standards. They are nevertheless very helpful in terms of the evidence they provide concerning details of monastic life or ritual practices. Having said that, we need to be careful even about such details. Documents like these can also give a false impression because they tend to work within strongly conventional patterns and so offer a misleading picture of uniformity within monastic life. The stories are, after all, mainly the products of successful, large, wealthy and often mixed religious settlements and tend to describe life within this kind of place. In reality, however, most monastic settlements were relatively small.

There are two features of the organisation of sacred space that were fairly similar across all sizes of settlement. First, the inner sanctum, or holy place, was clearly defined. Secondly, the overall religious space had an enclosing wall. Even the small hermitage of Cuthbert on the island of Inner Farne exhibited both features. Bede's *Life of Cuthbert* records that the saint built a small 'city of God', a *civitas*, fitted for his rule and within it houses suited to his city. This amounted to the bare essentials of an enclosure wall, a cell to live in, a place to pray and a place to be buried.[1]

Boundaries and Enclosure

The origins of some kind of boundary or enclosure for Christian religious or monastic sites are obscure but seem to go back to the earliest times. In the eastern Mediterranean the precinct walls of ancient Roman forts often acted as boundaries for the earliest monasteries. Where such facilities did not exist mud walls were deliberately erected. There were obviously practical reasons for this such as the protection of food cultivation from the weather and from animals or the defence of the inhabitants against robbers and other marauders. However, such boundaries also gave physical shape to the requirements of privacy as well as a sense of distinctive identity and separation from surrounding society.[2]

With some exceptions, Celtic religious sites favoured a circular plan. It was both the visible familiarity of circular designs in their culture and also the ancient symbolism of the circle that probably influenced Celtic monastic personnel. Amongst the familiar examples were the circles and spirals of traditional art, such as designs on metalwork or stones, and the numerous ring forts in the landscape. In terms of symbolism, the significance of circle designs on stones will be discussed later in more detail. At this point it is appropriate to note that the circle, because it has no discernible start or end point, was a powerful symbol of eternity and of spatial infinity. In other words, the circle represented created reality or the cosmos.

It would be foolish to pretend that circle symbolism was unique to Celtic culture or to its form of Christianity. We may recall the circular churches and baptisteries of the Mediterranean in late antiquity or the rose windows and labyrinth designs of some medieval cathedrals.[3] The main point here is that the circular design of Celtic religious sites undoubtedly suggested that such places were replicas of the cosmos, microcosms of the macrocosm. The circular boundary wall spoke eloquently of the desire of the inhabitants to create a place that existed simultaneously on two planes – the here and now and that of cosmic or universal reality.[4]

The boundaries of religious enclosures also marked off a

realm where spiritual powers, or the power of good, predominated over evil. Within the enclosure the rules of raw nature gave way to the sacred powers of ritual and prayer. Beyond the boundary wall lay a 'wilderness' that was not only naturally uncultivated and socially untamed but was also the dwelling place of demons and the forces of evil.[5]

In general, within the monastic 'space' of western Europe there took place a positive and creative meeting between various long-standing literary and artistic traditions and the Christian world-view. Celtic religious communities were places of cultural dialogue and encounter in even more specific ways. There, traditional sacred rituals were preserved (even if adapted), the great tradition of bardic education was maintained, local ties of kinship were expressed and political or legal structures were often centred. The 'monastery' was, in practice, a microcosm of the whole of society. The boundary wall should not therefore be thought of as a monastic *enclosure* in the later medieval sense. The latter unequivocally separated a particular group definitively from the everyday life of the rest of the Church or from society at large.

When it comes to interpreting Celtic religious sites or monasteries we need to transcend the spiritual polarities of 'worldliness' and 'withdrawal' that dominate many traditional histories of spirituality. Physical boundaries in the Celtic way of things often showed the interpenetration of religious and social relationships rather than the opposite. As we have already seen, in no other part of the western Church did monasticism, or at least monastic concepts, so dominate social life as well as spirituality as in the Celtic lands, particularly in Ireland. The kinship model of social relations continued to dominate and was closely associated with place. In this way of seeing things, 'place' in the geographical sense and a person's 'place in the world' were intimately connected. It is not surprising, therefore, that this same kinship structure of society also governed the ways in which religious enclosures and sacred spaces were organised. The passionate concern for kinship meant that people, including monastics, were judged by their ancestral line.

Basically, society was made up of lords and clients. So, when Celts, and especially the Irish, took God as supreme Lord this kind of relationship was clearly in mind. It is significant that one of the best-known groups of ascetics that arose in the ninth century were known as *celi de* (culdees) or 'clients of God'.

In the midst of agricultural enclosures and princely forts the tombs of saints (often of the same kin group) were planted and then guarded by monastic or clerical personnel. The central feature of Irish saints in particular is that they were people of power. Like Columba, many were from the aristocratic strata of society. They shared the general prestige with which people of learning, such as the druids, had been held. Some of the saints also seem to have inherited the traditional prophetic and vision-ary powers of the druids. A number may have been educated by druids. Presumably it is not beyond the realms of possibility that a few may once have been druids themselves. These various factors combined to build up a popular perception that saints were people of status and power. These saints who had arisen from within the people continued to mediate for the people with God even after (or, perhaps, especially after) their death. The religious personnel who continued to guard saintly graves were, therefore, seen as particularly able to facilitate people's access to God. This access came about through the performance of ritual and more generally through the Christian tradition of belief and practice being passed on. The larger Irish 'monastic' enclosures that we know of contained a fairly representative cross-section of society.[6]

Smaller, more ascetic, groups were obviously considerably more distinctive than the large mixed enclosures in relation to the population at large. In the larger enclosures there was often little practical distinction between the general population and clerical or monastic sub-groups. The exception to this generalis-ation was that clerics and monastics were often a social elite. Because of the ambiguities in the Celtic use of monastic termin-ology, it seems likely that people of both sexes were considered as 'monks' even if they lived within normal family life.

It would be inappropriate in this context to consider 'married monks' as evidence of spiritual decline or of the invasion of monastic ideals by an unseemly worldliness. The fact that monastic offices were held by successive members of family groups, many of whom were not clerics, reflects the reality that 'monasteries' and monastic concepts were ways of talking about the local Church. Everyone in the family was equally a part of the Church and its social world. Such a blurring of distinctions was unexceptionable when the gulf between social, general ecclesial and monastic structures was so narrow.

The ambiguities became more of a problem after the gradual imposition of more structured and supposedly 'reformed' monasticism in the High Middle Ages. An example would be the restructuring of the community on Iona under the Rule of St Benedict in the early years of the thirteenth century. The evidence from places like Iona suggests that the traditional family domination of monastic offices such as abbot or prior continued throughout the Middle Ages. New novices were also quite regularly granted dispensations from the impediment of being the son of a present or deceased monk. This has often been interpreted unequivocally as an appalling corruption of the monastic ideal but given the pre-history of the Benedictine Abbey at Iona such a negative view may need some refinement.[7]

Monastery as Sacred Space

Although, as we shall see, there were a variety of sub-divisions within the basic monastic space, the religious enclosure as a whole may also be considered as sacred space. The consecration and blessing of church buildings was common within western Christianity, but the blessing of Celtic religious sites seems to have been understood as possessing particularly strong powers. When Maedoc founded the monastic settlement of Druim Letham in the sixth century he is recorded as blessing the site, then marking out where its churches would be and arranging the boundary wall and the cemeteries. The act of consecration stated quite clearly that the chosen site existed in a sacred as well as a physical landscape with an attendant set of spiritual relations that needed to be properly ordered.

Such ritual blessings of religious sites were believed to be effective for domestic dwellings as well. A man living close to Ailbe's monastery at Imlech is said to have asked for a similar ritual of foundation to be conducted around his new house. Ailbe granted his request and the blessing promised that the house would be protected from rain, wind and abandonment. The sanctity of monastic boundaries was perceived as giving the same protection. In other words, all hostile elements were excluded and the positive powers of the place were also bound in.[8]

Such protective prayers of blessing for boundaries, whether of places or around individuals, were quite common in the Celtic tradition. They are almost certainly adaptations of pre-Christian rites. Although the forms differed, such prayers often involved blessings and signs of protection being made to all four quarters of the world, then to the earth and finally to the skies above. The Rule of Tallaght, for a version of the reformed ascetics known as *celi de*, not only contained liturgical offices but other devotional exercises. These included a striking protection blessing to be said in a quasi-liturgical way by the monastic community. The members of the community were enjoined to turn East first of all and then to recite the Our Father and the '*Deus in adjutorium* to *festina* [the opening phrase of the Divine Office] three times'. This was to be done with both hands raised to heaven and was to be followed by the sign of the cross made with the right hand. The process was repeated to the remaining three quarters of the world, then with their faces bent to the ground and finally with their faces turned upwards towards heaven.[9]

As we have seen, some kind of boundary wall (usually an earth bank) enclosed Celtic monastic settlements. It is significant that farmsteads and other settlements had similar protection. These were partly status symbols delineating the legal area belonging to a person. In the case of monastic settlements, the boundary also marked out a legal area that was, in this case, to be regarded as sacred. This enclosure, or *termon*, was to be a place free from all aggression. Violence was legally and absolutely excluded by this precinct. This was a specifically Celtic version of the more general acceptance throughout Christendom that monastic settlements were places of sanctuary. Because of this absence of violence, monastic and other religious settlements also functioned as a kind of bank in which valuables could be placed for safe-keeping. Some of them also served as the equivalent of an open prison. Large settlements had groups of penitents attached to them, some of whom had committed serious crimes against society, such as murder.[10]

As we saw earlier, such boundaries around religious sites did not really function as enclosures to shut out the world or to separate monastics from other Christians. Because of this relative lack of separation from local society at large the evidence is that solitaries or groups of celibate ascetics occupied a separate enclosure within the wider boundary. Sometimes small groups moved apart from such settlements to live in more remote locations. Overall, however, a religious enclosure was simply a privileged space within which a particular vision of the world could be lived out. Thus, monks in the tradition of Columbanus saw monastic settlements as anticipations of paradise in which the forces of division, violence and evil were excluded. Wild beasts were tamed and nature was regulated. The privileges of Adam and Eve in Eden, received from God but lost by the Fall, were reclaimed.

The living out of this vision of an alternative world involved all the people who were brought within the enclosed space. It was not something that concerned merely the 'professional' ascetics. The Columbanian tradition, for example, believed that all people were called from birth to the experience of contemplation. So, 'monastic' enclosures were places of spiritual experience and of non-violence and also places of education, wisdom and art. Within the enclosures there took place, ideally speaking, an integration of all elements of human life, as well as of all classes of human society. This approach contrasts favourably with the exclusive and impoverished understanding of enclosure as a means of protecting 'spiritual persons' from everyone else. This view came, in due course, to dominate the rest of the western tradition of spirituality.[11]

Spaces within Space

There was no regular layout of buildings around a rectangular cloister as in other western monastic traditions, nor an overall segregation of monastics or clergy from the general populace in the great monastic 'cities'. Even so, Celtic religious settlements did employ some internal zoning of the enclosed space to provide areas of lesser and greater privacy.[12]

Usually, there were one or more small churches, a graveyard, a standing cross or two, probably a separate abbot's dwelling, a *scriptorium* (where manuscripts were copied) and a collection of small huts where the monks lived either alone or in small groups. The general choice of sites and overall layout did not make neatness or standardisation possible. As we have already noted, there were different kinds of people who were described as 'monks'. However, while they may have inhabited distinct areas they frequently lived within the same overall enclosure. The monastic centre of Kells in Ireland appears to have been an integral part of local society. Charters relate the buying and selling of private property within the enclosure. There was a market and craftsmen were attached to the monastery. Kells was also a great education centre and its monastic school had a high reputation. The street pattern of the present town reflects the old monastery pattern. There were public areas and a specially sacred area (where, for example, there was a 'desert' for the ascetics) whose perimeter was marked by crosses.[13]

Church buildings within religious settlements were tiny by the standards of the rest of Europe. Of course, in the early period of Christian culture, monastic or quasi-monastic groups were themselves small – usually no more than ten or twelve people. The point is, however, that church buildings did not in general increase in size at the same time that the settlements expanded. By the seventh century people were divided into different worship groups. Hence churches multiplied in number rather than increased in dimensions. Even where churches were relatively large, they were sub-divided as at Kildare. Here there were three divisions. The sanctuary or chancel housed the bishop and senior clergy. This was partitioned from the nave which was itself divided longitudinally with married women and virgins on the left and priests and laymen on the right.

Church laws around the seventh century also appear to recognise different spaces within the overall sacred space of the 'monastic' enclosure. The most holy space contained the relics of the saints. There was another area for clergy and a third for laymen and all the women, monastic ascetics or not. As at Kells, the strict ascetics might live separately from the rest of the settlement. The *Annals of Ulster* for 1162 indicate that the beginnings of the twelfth-century reforms of monastic life in Ireland involved a move away from the old hereditary system and towards a greater 'professionalisation' of the clergy. This in turn meant that, as for example at Derry, a clear distinction was introduced between secular and religious buildings and areas. There was a total separation of ordinary houses from the area of the churches and a wall was built around 'the centre'. This created a special area of sanctuary.[14]

Types of Monastic Personnel

The organisation of monastic space had obvious connections with the different types of people who inhabited the enclosure. In her study of Kells, Maire Herbert notes that there was a distinct 'disert' within the enclosure inhabited by a community of *celi de*. These may have had specific responsibility for ritual and liturgy within a larger and more broadly based monastic settlement. The total settlement represented a fusion of traditional social organisation and religious life.[15]

Not all the people within a sacred enclosure led celibate or explicitly ascetical lives. Space for monastic settlements had often been provided by whole kin groups. Some of its members then led an ascetical life and formed the inner circle of Church officers including the abbot or abbess and the bishops. Some settlements were more traditionally monastic in that they included only celibate ascetics but most of the larger ones also included *manaig* who married and farmed the land. This implied that some 'monastic' personnel (perhaps the majority in some settlements) were born into the system. The *manaig* were not tenants but within the 'monastic' family. It is true that it is perhaps less helpful to think of settlements as monasteries in our traditional understanding of the word. However, there is evidence that some married, non-clerical *manaig* became abbots or the overall leader of the religious settlement. The *manaig* had a spiritual regime although the law tracts concerning them that are appended, for example, to the Rule of Tallaght speak of men, women, boys and girls. This clearly implies normal family life.

A 'monastic' enclosure, therefore, was a settlement dedicated to religious purposes but within which comparatively few lived a strictly ascetical life. In this sense, the large 'monastic' settlements were really the local Church, a microcosm of the Church Universal. In terms of sacred space, *manaig* lived fully within the enclosure, had the right to attend certain rituals within the church but also had to undertake some degree of ascetical behaviour that was not expected of other Christians who lived outside the enclosure.[16]

Men and Women

In the case of the *manaig* who were married, there were clearly no domestic divisions between men and women. But what of the monastic enclosures as a whole? Were men and women segregated? Were there restrictions on women within sacred enclosures? The evidence is ambiguous.

The famous story of Brigit at Kildare who talked to the visiting monastic student in the refectory concerning the death of his soul friend implies that even celibate men and women could share the same eating space. Kildare, of course, was itself a double monastery of men and women.[17] *Candida Casa* (Whithorn) in South West Scotland had a strong double monastery early in the sixth century and many Irish monastics spent years training there. It appears that this may be the origin of the later foundation of double monasteries in Ireland (for example,

Kildare) and Northumbria (for example, Whitby). Kildare was the most famous Irish monastic settlement led by women. The nuns were not strictly enclosed and lived alongside clerics with a bishop in their midst. Under the leadership of Ite, the monastic settlement of Killeedy seems to have been based on kinship groups. It had married nuns with children and functioned as a mixed group of clerics and lay, men and women, married and celibate, just like some of the male-led communities.

Later in the eighth century Bede, a celibate Northumbrian Benedictine, in his *Ecclesiastical History* hints that Coldingham in Northumbria fell on bad times because there was no effective separation between the sexes in a double settlement. Yet at the same time he spoke highly of Whitby under Hilda which was also a double house in which, from archaeological evidence, there does not seem to have been a rigid segregation of the sexes.

Not all monastic writers were pro-women. It seems that there may have been only four major Irish monastic settlements where women had a prominent role, that is, Kildare, Killeedy, Killevy and Clonbroney. The Life of Senan suggests that women sometimes had to struggle pretty hard to be allowed to share life as equals within a monastic enclosure. So one woman is reported to have argued to Senan: 'Christ is no worse than you. Christ came to save women no less than men. He suffered for women no less than men. Women have given service in the mystery to Christ and his apostles. Women enter the heavenly kingdom no less than men.'[18]

Guests and Outsiders

So far we have examined only what might be thought of as 'insiders' within the monastic enclosures. But there were also various categories of short- or long-term visitors. What formal education that existed in Ireland was provided by the monastic settlements. Some of the students were the children of the *manaig* but Bede, for example, implies that famous masters attracted pupils from far away. It seems that some settlements, such as the island of Nendrum in Northern Ireland, had 'schools'

43

in distinct buildings. In others the individual monks taught students in their cells and pupils even boarded with them, thus living in the heart of the monastic space. This carried on the great tradition of druidic and bardic 'colleges' and culture. It may even be that one of the motives behind the development of such large monastic settlements was to accommodate pupils in sufficient numbers for 'schools' to flourish.[19]

There were also other passing guests to be accommodated. It seems that these were accorded a kind of semi-spiritual status and housed within the sacred enclosure. Often the guest house was given the choicest site within the settlement and yet was always set apart, sometimes within its own enclosure. The *hospitium*, therefore, was within the sacred space (isolated from the outside world) yet separated from the monastic living quarters. The guest quarters was itself, therefore, a kind of 'boundary place' between two worlds.[20]

Space for Solitude

If monastic settlements existed within boundaries that marked the whole as a kind of sacred space, there were differing degrees of sacred association. Although the overall pattern of settlements was to bring together social and religious structures, the more ascetical individuals and groups were to a greater or lesser degree set apart from the remainder of the inhabitants.

Absolutely solitary living was almost unknown in ordinary Celtic society for reasons of warmth, safety and scarcity of usable space. To opt for a solitary life – even just by living in personal sleeping quarters – was thus unique to monastic settlements. In the context it would have represented a distinctly ascetical rather than luxurious option. In fact most monastic personnel did not live alone but in huts of at least two people. It was not unusual for one to be the spiritual guide of the other and indeed the *anamchara*, or soul friend, implies 'one who shares the cell'.

It may well be that it was in the context of this asceticism of solitude that the notion of private penance (leading eventually to the practice of confession) developed. In such a communal society, where social and religious structures intermingled so strongly, it may have been that some degree of physical solitude was the only way of marking out those who sought a spiritual life-style that was distinguishable from that of the overall religious settlement.[21]

Conclusion

In summary, the enclosed space of religious sites was a kind of microcosm of the cosmos in its concept of harmony and proper relationship. By the standards of other western religious enclosures, the Celtic sites seem disordered and haphazard. However, there was an inner logic not only to the overall shape of the enclosures but also to the relationship of buildings, groups of inhabitants and internal boundary markers such as crosses. Despite appearances, this was a highly ordered world. In it humans, animals, natural features and the spiritual realm were brought into an appropriate relationship with each other by means of the various physical boundaries that were employed.

FOUR

Marking Spiritual Boundaries

As we have already seen, the spirituality of Celtic Christianity, inherited from its pre-Christian origins, included an extraordinary sense that the 'other world', of saints, the dead, angels, demons and God, was close at hand. The boundaries between this material world and that other world were all around people. Human beings live permanently in a world that is a boundary place. Nevertheless, particular locations were considered to have a special quality of liminality or to be especially sacred because of their associations. It was common for the Celts to mark these special boundaries in tangible ways.

Many of the major religious sites in Celtic lands are notable because of the presence of standing crosses or the importance of the burial site associated with the settlement. This is because both crosses and cemeteries have a special significance in relation to living on the boundary between the two worlds of material reality and of the spirit.

Origin and Role of High Crosses

Celtic Christianity rarely produced large churches or outstanding religious architecture in comparison to the other lands of western Christendom. It is great, free-standing, three-dimensional or 'high' crosses rather than buildings that stand out in the landscape. These crosses are also among the most striking monuments of Christian religious symbolism in the Celtic lands. Crosses exist particularly in Ireland where the total runs to about a hundred but are also to be found in North and West Britain. The crosses are undoubtedly a major contribution to early Christian art in general. Yet, in the context of their own time and place, the importance of the High Crosses was far greater than mere decoration. This, of course, would be true of all major examples of western religious art and architecture. Art was certainly an act of worship, probably imbued with arcane symbolism. Art may also have had a didactic purpose even if experts are nowadays more cautious about asserting without further qualification that medieval wall paintings or windows were simply 'the poor man's bible'.

Because Wales had been part of the Roman Province of Britain, and had in part been Christianised in the later years of the Empire, many of the earliest surviving standing stones with Christian associations come from there and date from as early as the fifth century.[1] However, the custom of free-standing crosses seems to be a ninth-century import. The age of the great Irish crosses dates from the eighth century onwards when the cult of Jesus' crucifixion, inspired by Mediterranean art and the Roman liturgy, spread north across Europe. However, it would seem that these influences combined with already existing Irish Christian traditions concerning the importance of cross symbolism and ritual. So, for example, Adomnan's *Life of Columba* refers to the constant use of the sign of the cross.[2]

Despite the obvious connection between the cross and the central doctrines of the Christian faith, it seems likely that its popularity among the Celts also reflects values and a symbolism that predate the Christian era. We have already seen that boundary blessings, adapted from pre-Christian rituals, not only involved making the sign of the cross with the hand but took place in a cross-shaped pattern facing to the four points of the compass. Four points, or a cross, suggests a cosmic symbolism that is probably also reflected in the peculiar combination of cross and circle in the High Cross designs.

The most obvious point about a High Cross, apart from the cross itself, is that it is a pillar or standing stone whose vertical axis is dominant. Pillar stones were present in Celtic lands long before Christianity arrived. The earliest carved stones were frequently natural ones with inscriptions or designs marked on them. Originally the stones probably symbolised the *axis mundi* or the pole that was understood to form a link between earth and heaven. These pillar stones in turn almost certainly replaced sacred trees at a time when the Celtic people, who had previously been nomadic, began to settle and to clear land for agriculture.

Both Roman writing about the Gauls and early Irish texts throw an interesting light on the importance of the sacred tree (*bile*) among the Celts.[3] In other cultures, vertical totems of various kinds were frequently placed at the centre of tribal villages. The traditional English maypole (which may have a similar significance) was usually erected in a central location on the village green. This reminds us that the *axis mundi* not only marked a vertical link between heaven and earth but was also the centre of reality, of the world itself.

In his important study of the connection between British church sites and the landscape, Richard Morris suggests that the High Crosses were the product of what he calls 'a moment of religio-cultural elision'. That is to say, an already existing tradition of pillar monuments and the new imagery of the redemptive death of Christ fused together.

On this theory, the Celtic cross is a Christianised *axis mundi* – the 'sacred tree' that links heaven and earth; the centre and source out of which all blessings flow. At times this process of religious fusion may even have involved the 'Christianisation' of already existing standing stones. So, for example, a seventh-century life of St Samson in Cornwall describes how the saint found pagans dancing around a stone and then how, after converting them, he simply marked the stones with crosses. The pillar stone at Llangernyw in North Wales has nothing more than a small incised cross on it. Without this, the pillar could easily be a typical pre-Christian *menhir* or standing stone.[4] In South Wales particularly, the free-standing crosses were often composite in structure. That is to say, they were made up of several distinct pieces of stone with the actual cross head carved separately from the shaft. This seems to emphasise a progressive development from a simple standing stone to one with a cross placed on top of it.[5]

Having said this, it needs to be added that the Celtic lands were not isolated places totally disconnected from other European cultural influences. The designs of the especially fine crosses that appeared from the mid-eleventh century are often creative reinterpretations of both Scandinavian and continental Roman-esque motifs.[6]

The second obvious feature of cross stones is that they possessed a specific Christian meaning. If we ask what the purpose of the crosses was, the clearest answer is that they existed simply to testify to the Christian faith. In this context something else important to be said about crosses is that they were decorated. What is not so clear is whether it is the decoration or the location of the crosses that is more significant! Although, as we shall see, many of the designs were abstract ones or based on natural objects, there were also illustrations of biblical stories. These may have served to feed the imagination in a prayerful or catechetical way. In fact there is evidence that the crosses were used as places for meditation or perhaps for outdoor preaching – sermons or prayers in stone as some authorities have called them.[7] At least one monastic rule suggests that the crosses served as places for penitential exercises: 'at the cross with humility, without disputes, let each confess his faults there'.[8]

The location of the crosses was also important. Some marked places of special events, especially those associated with the founder of the particular religious community. However, the most common purpose seems to have been to mark boundaries of various kinds. Thus it is common for crosses to appear at the entrances and exits of the religious enclosures and, as at Iona, to mark internal thresholds such as the entrance to church buildings. Internal divisions within the overall enclosure of religious settlements also had crosses, especially the boundaries of the particularly sacred places. Eighth-century Church laws established that such signs should ritually divide the less sacred areas from the *termon* or 'holy area' where the more ascetical members of communities lived. Thus, a circle of crosses often came to mark what was in effect the 'cloister'.[9] 'Let the place that shelters me amidst monastic enclosures be a beautiful spot hallowed by [holy] stones, and I all alone therein.'[10]

Because the Celtic perception of 'place' and landscape was not a purely material one, the marking of boundaries was also not merely practical. Crosses marked what might be called cosmic entrance and exit points where the material world and the world of the spirit were believed to come into especially close contact. It is not surprising, therefore, that crosses are sited frequently at the entrances to burial places which, because of their association with death and resurrection, marked the most dramatic boundary place of all.

Rings and Spirals

The ringed or disc-headed stone cross was particularly distinctive of the Celtic lands and also spread to parts of Anglo-Danish England before the Norman Conquest. The combination of ringed head and standing cross became the best-known type and in Ireland, for example, the ring achieved an almost universal significance. These most famous crosses enclosed the actual cross within a circle. Although Welsh crosses were eventually influenced considerably by Irish decoration, the distinctive Welsh cross tended to be a disc head rather than ringed in the strict sense.[11]

The origin of ringed crosses has been much discussed and it seems unlikely that there will ever be a definitive answer. Indeed, it is probable that there is no single reason for their development. If so, questions of their symbolic value must also be complex rather than simple. There are likely to have been both practical and specifically Christian reasons for the rings. What follows is, therefore, fairly speculative.

A practical interpretation indicates that as the design developed from a cross symbol carved on a simple stone shaft to the actual shape of a cross placed at the top, it became necessary to place extra pieces of stone in order to brace the horizontal arms. If we look at the development in terms of Christian symbolism, a number of alternative suggestions have been made. There is perhaps some association with a halo or nimbus given that this became generally widespread in representations of Christ from the fourth century onwards, especially in the East. The putative connections between Celtic Christianity and the eastern Mediterranean seem to be reinforced by the suggestion that there was a Coptic inspiration for the ringed crosses in Egyptian circled faces of the crucified Christ. There also seems to have been a close formal resemblance to Byzantine representations of the cross. These included a crown of thorns, designed as a wreath, around its centre.[12]

One of the most favoured explanations nowadays is that the ringed crosses represent an adaptation of the Chi-Rho monogram, which consisted of the first two letters of the Greek word for the name of Christ. It was not the cross but the *labarum*, the Chi-Rho surrounded by a wreath of victory, that the Emperor Constantine was supposed to have used on his standard at the battle of the Milvian Bridge in 312 CE. It seems that during the late fourth and fifth centuries the simple Chi-Rho developed so that the X became gradually rotated until one stroke coincided with the down stroke of the P. Then the curved part of the P became gradually detached and followed round to create a circle enclosing what is now a +. Some authorities have added that a Chi-Rho within a circle may be a symbol of resurrection and eternal life.[13]

The notion that circle or ringed crosses have a connection with the theme of eternal life or eternity brings us back once again to Celtic concepts of place and especially the boundaries between this world and the 'other' world of divine, angelic and spiritual beings. The ring on the cross is also a wheel. Wheels in pre-Christian designs frequently symbolise a repeating cycle where beginning and end coincide. All that exists is bound to rise and then fall in turn. This sense of the cyclic pattern of existence, both of nature and human life, is quite likely maintained as one aspect among many in the popularity of ringed crosses.[14]

The moving wheel also has the powerful capacity to symbolise God. God is the still point with no dimensions at the centre, around which all else moves. This hub or centre may be thought of as a specific place. It nevertheless includes, as it were, everything else – the whole world. It is the place that connects us to all places. A ring or wheel around a cross is particularly striking in this regard as the geometry of cross and wheel was used in pre-Christian sites and designs to symbolise both the four seasons and the four points of the world. Thus calendar and compass, time and place, are combined in the union of cross and wheel.[15]

Even if the ring on the cross does derive partly from the Byzantine nimbus or halo, it has been pointed out that the nimbus itself may derive from an ancient solar symbol. St Patrick's *Confessio* or *Declaration*, chapter 60, suggests that all who worship the perishable sun are doomed and that the sun must give way to the true Sun, 'Christ who will never perish'.[16] Druidic religion was sun-related. Whether through the Byzantine nimbus or via a specifically Celtic elision of traditional and Christian images of the divine, it seems feasible that the juxtaposition of circle and cross involved a superimposition of the Son of God on the Sun God.[17]

Such symbolism of universal place, eternity and divinity is also reinforced by the fact that the ring shape on the cross resembles the endless spirals so favoured in Celtic art. These appear not only on metalwork and manuscripts, such as the Book of Kells, but also on many of the crosses themselves. Spirals, like circles, are designs without identifiable beginning or end. Again this would be a particularly appropriate and powerful design at those boundary places between worlds where crosses were commonly placed. Within the circular boundary of settlements, perhaps marked with crosses, and within areas 'marked' by circle blessings the powers of chaos and darkness were thought to be excluded. This seems to relate to a traditional Celtic belief that evil powers were frustrated by any shape that did not have a definite start or finish. It may follow that a circle combined with a cross, the specific Christian symbol of redemption, would suggest an even more potent barrier against the powers of darkness. So a circle or a spiral was also a protection. It is also rather obviously a symbol of movement or journey – the dialectical opposite of 'place' yet intimately connected with it.

The spatial conventions of some of the tales of Celtic ascetic wanderers are interesting and reinforce the sense that the circle motif is intimately related to journeying, especially sacred journeys. So, for example, the *Navigatio Brendani* presents an understanding of space that is beyond the experience of everyday life. Brendan's 'voyage' moves not in a line but in a circular fashion. The cyclical quality is both physical, moving round the four points of the compass, and liturgical. The voyagers spend the significant religious holy days of the yearly cycle at locations apparently specified by God through an angelic messenger. This cyclical quality of the voyage reminds the reader that the journey is an internal, spiritual one.

> Brendan's course is a circle. It is repetitive, inevitable, preordained, but nevertheless salvific. The ineluctable rise and fall of human existence is rendered salutary when Brendan achieves his goal and arrives at the Promised Land of the Saints.[18]

Circles and spirals were almost certainly associated with the journey from physical existence through death to eternal life. It has been noted that spiral symbolism was common at prehistoric graves. For example, at Newgrange in Northern Ireland there were spirals particularly at the entrance–exit doorway through which it was believed the spirit of the deceased would pass from time-bound existence into eternity. The spiral patterns form a kind of maze, possibly representing a 'guide' to the spirit passing out of this world into the other world or acting as a metaphor of the human life-journey in general.[19]

The maze or labyrinth design reappears quite explicitly in Christian forms as well. Glendalough in County Wicklow preserves a well-defined pilgrim road. At one point there was a great granite boulder, now in the National Museum in Dublin, which is decorated quite clearly with a labyrinth and which stood close to the old road. At one time this stone was interpreted as pagan but its proximity to the pilgrim route is now taken to indicate a connection with the sacred Christian site of Glendalough.[20]

To suggest that there was a link between such designs and the conception of a sacred journey is not so strange. After all, labyrinth designs similarly appear in medieval cathedrals – on the floor as at Chartres, or exactly the same design on an archway pillar outside the great West door at Lucca Cathedral in Tuscany. Some people have suggested that these too were pagan symbols adapted to Christian use. In the case of Chartres, it was thought that penitents walked the labyrinth on their knees as a kind of symbolic representation of pilgrimage to the holy places of Palestine. Here, too, as at the pre-Christian site of Newgrange, the journey represented is not simply one of pilgrimage to a holy place, Glendalough or Jerusalem. Commentators on the Chartres labyrinth, for example, write of it as a symbol of the human journey towards a *celestial* Jerusalem. In other words, it was the path of the soul through life. The Glendalough labyrinth, like that of Chartres and others, has only one route to the centre, to God, to enlightenment, to completion. This was very different from the spider's web of enticing false paths that characterised the later Renaissance mazes. In the earlier labyrinths the symbolic purpose was different. If you kept going far and long enough on your pilgrimage inwards you necessarily reached the centre. Perseverance was the key. It may be, too, that the layers of concentric circles in labyrinths reflect idealised models of the universe, a microcosm of the macrocosm, an image of Creation.[21]

Burial Places

The reference to the megalithic grave at Newgrange brings us to the importance of burial places in Celtic thinking, whether Christian or earlier. Like crosses, cemeteries were important symbols of the boundary between this world and the other world that was always close at hand. In fact, in both pre-Christian and Christian forms, the world of the dead was not so much another world as another region, or dimension, of this world. Places of burial could give access to this region. So, as we shall see in the next chapter, might sea journeys.[22]

Many of the important 'monastic' settlements were focused around the burial place of the saintly founder of the *paruchia*, or 'family' of the saint. The guiding and sustaining presence of the saint was not merely linked to a specific place but also to the relics that remained. Thus, when some of Iona's relics of

Columba were taken to Kells in Ireland to avoid further Viking depredations, the *praesentia*, or living presence, of Columba transferred itself to the new setting. A cemetery was not simply the shrine of the founding saint but was also 'the place of resurrection' – a doorway from time into eternity in a special way. Burial places were, and still are in Ireland, sites where the membrane between two worlds is felt to be very thin. The organisation of the monastic enclosure was closely related to the tomb of the founder. In a physical, as well as a metaphorical, sense the settlement centred on the saint. Access to the holy place and to the saint, via the relics, was jealously guarded and was not open to everyone. Internal walls, a cross or a series of them isolated this holiest of sacred spaces.[23]

There can be no doubt that one important factor in why some monastic sites, 'the little places settled by twos and threes', had become *civitates* or major settlements by about 800 was whether the place possessed the tomb of a saint. This was not simply because it acted as a powerful focus for the maintenance of an effective Church organisation. The burial place was also hallowed ground and other people, not least the nobility, were keen to be buried alongside the saints, thus bringing burial fees and wealth. Because the early medieval Celtic Christians could see burial grounds as gateways to the other life, over which angels dwelt and from which there was passage to the land of the saints, they were great places of visiting and pilgrimage. Within the life of the religious community and the surrounding society, the cemeteries played a significant role. For example, vows could be pronounced there or oaths taken. On Iona, the ritual casting of lots (*sortilegia*) continued on a cross stump in the graveyard even beyond the Reformation.[24]

The continuity of religious sites associated with burial places, particularly but not exclusively in Ireland, is quite remarkable. The building of churches is obviously closely connected to burial sites. As cemeteries were some of the earliest, and most common, stable Christian sites they attracted small churches within them that eventually became popular chapels or even parish churches. In Ireland, Catholic burials continue unabated in Protestant churchyards if the burial ground is an early one with a long tradition. Many of the ancient grave sites are still in use and in some cases span some fifteen hundred years.[25] Many of the old saintly sites are still used for pilgrimage too. On the saint's festival the crowds gather and the cemetery is tidied up. An interesting link between pilgrimages and cemeteries is recalled in the Irish word *romh* or *ruamh* which means 'holy burial ground' but which derives from *Roma* or Rome, an archetypal place of pilgrimage.[26]

Another fascinating continuity of language and place exists throughout the Celtic Christian world in reference to burial places. The late British word for an enclosure was *landa*. Derivatives of this were used for burial grounds, then for their contents and finally for the social and religious settlements that sprang up around them. So in Wales we have the word *Llan* in numerous place names and in Cornwall, *Lan*. In Ireland and Scotland there was a parallel development. There the word was *Kill* or *Cill* derived from the Latin *Cella*. In Manx the equivalent was *Keeill*. This may have referred originally to a small, marked-out compartment of land with religious significance. Alternatively it might refer to the ascetic's cell attached to a church which itself was sometimes associated with a burial place. In any case 'cell' underlies hundreds of Irish place names such as Kildare, Killarney, Killiney and so on.

Conclusion

Boundary places seem to exercise a universal fascination. In England the meeting place of counties (especially if more than two come together in one place) is often marked by a name, an inn or some other sign. In my own home county of Dorset, there are many ancient sunken lanes which are still walked and which are carefully protected. These arose as boundary ditches between the lands of different ancient settlements or of early manors. Elsewhere in Europe I recall the excitement of a group of children at being able to stand on top of a Pyrenean mountain with one foot in France and the other in Spain! When the boundary is thought to be between the world of everyday experience and that of spiritual realities the fascination is even more potent. It is not too extreme to suggest that the Celtic Christians had a kind of mystical sense of boundaries which is why they so often marked them with religious symbols and rituals.

FIVE

Pilgrimage and Journey

A striking paradox of Celtic spirituality is that on the one hand early British Christianity had a strongly developed sense of place and kinship connections while on the other it developed a peculiar form of wandering asceticism. The love of wandering, *peregrinatio* or pilgrimage, is indeed one of the most original features of Celtic Christianity. As we shall see, this 'pilgrimage' theme was interpreted in both a literal and a figurative sense.

Motives for Wandering

The extraordinary development of wandering asceticism in Celtic Christianity has perhaps three sources. In a general way the notion of a sacred journey is present in many religious cultures and mythologies across the globe and throughout history. Modern writers such as Bruce Chatwin have suggested that our natural inclination as human beings turns us to movement and journeying. We are born to be nomads.[1] This view may be an exaggeration, born of a certain rootlessness in late-twentieth-century western culture. Nevertheless, there is some truth in the idea that humans are naturally attracted to journeys.

If we turn our attention to the specifically religious or spiritual dimension of life, it is noticeable that many people in all cultures go on pilgrimage in search of a special place associated with ultimate fulfilment or eternal life. In ancient myth, such a place would also be associated with human origins. It may be where the ancestors or gods came from. It may be the place of creation or it may be paradise. Whether one or all of these elements is present, the search was for a place of special theophany and therefore of renewal. In this sense, the physical journey was the acting out of an inner journey. This is what differentiates it from aimless wandering or modern tourism.

The second source for Celtic journeying is specifically Christian. Throughout the history of Christian spirituality religious explorers have sought a home in some form of 'desert'. This could not always be a literal desert. The distinctive island geography of Britain produced a unique form of the 'desert ascetic' – the spiritual seafarer. Wandering by sea was hardly unique to the Celts. The Anglo-Saxon poem 'The Seafarer' indicates some development of the same pilgrim theme among other cultural groups in the British Isles.[2] However, beyond the British Isles, the Norse seafarers, even when Christianised, did not seem to develop a similar theory or practice of seascape asceticism.

In the Celtic, especially Irish, way of seeing such matters, the ultimate point of spiritual wandering was to 'seek the place of one's resurrection'. This involved seeking to enter the Kingdom of God more easily by means of living in the world as a stranger for Christ's sake. The 'place of resurrection' was the place appointed by God for the particular wanderer to settle and spend the remaining years of life doing penance and waiting for death.

It is significant that this special, appointed place was not determined by tribe or culture but by God alone. This acted as a symbolic counterpoise to the Celtic attachment to clan and inherited landscape. Celtic spirituality offers a tension between attachment to place (and inheritance) and ascetical detachment by means of journey. Ultimately the ascetic tradition suggested that human existence could not be accepted passively as something given or stable. The call was to cast oneself upon the mystery of God symbolised by the uncontrolled and unpredictable elements of sea and wind. While pilgrimage in various forms was prevalent in medieval Christianity as a whole, this particular understanding and spirituality of it was not.[3]

It is worth mentioning that although we tend to associate pilgrimage with the Irish ascetics it seems that the Church in Wales had such a concept from early days. The category of *peregrinus* was the most numerous among the early Welsh ascetics, that is between the fifth and seventh centuries.[4]

While a penitential motive for undertaking pilgrimage was not unique to Celtic Christianity, it was certainly particularly prominent. It also seems that the penitential pilgrimage, to expiate sin or to discipline the body, may have been an Irish invention, developed from as early as the sixth century.

> A dear pure pilgrimage
> subduing faults, a body chaste,
> a life of poverty lowly and secluded
> occur often to my mind.
>
> The gift of piety, the gift of pilgrimage
> the gift of repentance for my soul,
> O Christ without reproach,
> grant them all to me.[5]

The desert tradition of monastic life, by which Celtic, especially Irish, spirituality may have been influenced, placed a central emphasis on the importance of staying in one place, specifically the 'cell', in order to find God. The point was stressed that if one could not find God in stability, there was no guarantee that God could be experienced by moving anywhere else. Stability in itself was also a protection against seeking to assuage spiritual boredom by wandering hither and thither. 'Gyrovagues', or wandering ascetics, were viewed with suspicion by later monastic rules such as that of St Benedict in the west.

> Fourth and finally, there are the monks called gyrovagues, who spend their entire lives drifting from region to region, staying as guests for three or four days in different monasteries. Always on the move, they never settle down, and are slaves to their own wills and gross appetites.[6]

Even in the Celtic tradition, steadiness, perseverance and spiritual stability were emphasised. Those who sought to wander were liable to be challenged in order to test the quality of their desires. Thus a teacher named Dairchellach was challenged by the virgin Samhthann.

> 'I wish to go across the sea in pilgrimage', he said. She replied: 'If God could not be found on this side of the sea we would indeed journey across. Since, however, God is nigh unto all who call upon Him, we are under no obligation to cross the sea. The kingdom of heaven can be reached from every land.'[7]

At best, the Celtic spiritual wanderers combined an inner stability or constancy of vision and purpose with an outward mobility.

Columbanus (c.543–615), the great Celtic monastic founder and wanderer across much of western Europe, employed 'road' and 'journey' as his favoured metaphors for the Christian life. Life itself was a roadway that led to eternity.

> Let us concern ourselves with things divine, and as pilgrims ever sigh for and desire our homeland; for the end of the road is ever the object of travellers' hopes and desires, and thus, since we are travellers and pilgrims in the world, let us ever ponder on the end of the road, that is of our life, for the end of our roadway is our home.[8]

The old Irish *Life of Columba* (to be distinguished from Adomnan's *Life*) also suggests that pilgrimage is of the essence of Christianity rather than merely an eccentric practice of some ascetics.

> God counselled Abraham to leave his own country and go in pilgrimage into the land which God has shown him, to wit the 'Land of Promise' . . . Now the good counsel which God enjoined here on the father of the faithful is incumbent on all the faithful; that is to leave their country and their land, their wealth and their worldly delight for the sake of the Lord of the Elements, and go in perfect pilgrimage in imitation of him.[9]

Origins of the Sacred Journey

The third source of the 'journey' metaphor stems from a pre-Christian voyage tradition. The earlier journeys to The Land of Promise and rebirth elide eventually with the Christian ideal of seeking the place of resurrection. There is a great tradition of Irish voyage tales, the *echtra* ('outing') or the *immrama* ('rowing about'), where the interest is in the journey itself and not merely on its end point or purpose.

The most famous is the Voyage of Bran (on which it is likely that the Brendan Voyage is modelled) dating probably from the seventh century. Bran journeys into the ocean with his companions from somewhere in the West of Ireland, probably Kerry, after hearing a song of the delights of the other world.[10]

In the pre-Christian Celtic tradition the world of the dead was simply a happier replica of this world. The soul was immortal and could travel far from its native land to mysterious and legendary islands. Among the names given to this world were Island of Women, Land of the Living, Land of Youth, Land of Promise, Land of Joy. This land had no tempests and no excess of heat or cold. There were no dangerous animals. The Land of Eternal Youth was unvisited by death or disease and was in an eternal springtime where fruit and flowers grew without labour.

It was not difficult to connect these traditional motifs with Christian ideas of resurrection and eternal life. The tendency to refer to such a 'land' as being in the west probably relates to the direction of the setting sun. So, far in the west was the divine land where the Sun God rested. There is a close relationship between elements found in the voyage of Bran (which may in any case have partly Christian inspiration) and that of Brendan. A general continuity of ideas and even ideals between pre-Christian and Christian journeys is not impossible. The monastic voyage tales also have the saints and their companions seek the Land of Promise on some island in the ocean. Apart from the specifically Christian imagery, these saints have all the qualities of ancient pagan heroes.[11]

The stories of the Voyage of Brendan seem to have been known around the year 800. A Litany of Saints from that period has three allusions to it. The famous *Navigatio Brendani* probably dates from later in the ninth century, c.850, even though the saint lived from c.500–c.583. It has a simple plot but blends pre-Christian journey traditions, folklore, Christian legend, a strong narrative, poetry and monastic imagery.[12] Whatever the blend of images, motifs and ideas, it is generally agreed that the story as a whole reflects Irish monastic society and ideals. Interesting attempts have been made to prove that there really was such a voyage by the monk St Brendan (in which he may even have reached the North American coast). However, it is probably more crucial to the interpretation of the tale to see it as a parable of the spiritual-monastic inner journey.

So, the monks whom Brendan encounters on the *insula deliciosa* live in separate huts (expressing a connection between the pilgrimage tradition and the inner journey of the hermit life). They follow a vegetarian diet but say the Divine Office and eat together. Brendan's voyage is accompanied by many sensuous delights: a wonderful fragrance, shining light, singing birds and marvellous foods. However, the purpose was to seek 'the Land of Promise of the saints' and the attraction was to be 'where Christ is our light'.[13]

Not all pilgrimage was across the sea. There was also much wandering over the countryside, sometimes alone, sometimes with a small band of followers. In stopping places, perhaps a few small huts and a preaching cross were set up but frequently, after each settlement, some people kept on the move. It has been noticed, in reference especially to Wales, that it is possible to plot the sphere of influence of particular monastic saints and their followers from the distribution of churches bearing their name, although we need to be cautious about asserting too much.[14]

In a sense, the *peregrinatio* of the Celtic ascetics, whatever form it took, was always a journey to the 'other world'. There was sometimes a mystical as well as a mythical quality to the language for what the saints sought was no less than the land of Heaven itself. So, the Vision of Adamnan suggests that, 'The saints have need of nothing but to be listening to the music to which they listen and to look on the light which they see, and to be filled with the fragrance which is in the land.'[15] This land could be reached only by those 'who desire God'. The journey was through six lower heavens. There was a process of purgation involved for which the observance of monastic rules provided a means for the journey.

In the Christian era, for more than five hundred years, a stream of dedicated people poured out of the Celtic monasteries, mainly of Ireland and Scotland, to go on pilgrimage *pro Christo*, for Christ. The greatest heroes of Irish monasticism, the male ones at least such as Brendan, Columba and Columbanus, were vagrants. The specific end was immediately 'the place of resurrection' but eventually heaven. This was more important than any particular route and so ascetics often appeared to wander aimlessly. However, in their own minds they felt themselves to be divinely led, while being tossed hither and thither on the waves of the ocean. Yet, in fact, there are *patterns* of Celtic monastic journeys and settlements and this makes the stated philosophy 'we wandered wherever the winds took us without a rudder' seem rather disingenuous! There were certainly particular routes along which succeeding generations journeyed.[16]

Most of the pilgrims journeyed on their own initiative although mainly with the consent of their monastic leaders. There do not appear to have been many prolonged crises of decision. Response to a God-given imperative seems to have been prompt, often inspired by the Genesis text of the call of Abraham (12:1) to step out from the familiar place and to journey to a land chosen and revealed by God alone. The absoluteness of this sense of call was marked by the fact that the majority of such pilgrims typically never communicated again with home or kin.[17]

Effectively, the Celtic wanderers countered one of their deepest cultural instincts – an attachment to the home turf. They sentenced themselves to a perpetual banishment. This *peregrinatio* was not a sign of collective Celtic instability. The motivations were complex. Columbanus is said to have been provoked to leave his homeland because he was pursued by 'lascivious maidens'. For many it may have been a form of penance, both in a general ascetical sense and in reparation for specific crimes. In fact, it seems that the notion of going in a boat without rudder or oars, whether genuinely practised or not, may have derived from Irish legal practices inflicted on expelled criminals.

Enforced exile was used as a treatment for society's worst crimes. This was especially true of crimes against kin or against the prince for such crimes were particularly harmful to the cohesion of the community. There is a hint in traditions about Columba that while his pilgrimage to Iona may have been *pro*

Christo it might also have had something to do with his role in a civil war in Ulster. Those expelled from the enclosure into the wilderness faced the full force of the weather and joined the wild beasts and the demons.

The form of self-imposed exile was obviously different from active expulsion and yet may have been related in some ways. It was a form of punishment, albeit self-inflicted, in response to a deep sense of sin.

> We went on our pilgrimage
> At the blast of the whistling wind
> To obtain forgiveness of our sins
> There is the cause of asking.[18]

The ascetic went freely away from protection and out into the wild to the place of demons to combat them and to the place of wild beasts to wrestle with sensual appetites. The real test of faith was to turn one's back on the security of kin. The abandonment of homeland, friends, original religious community, and above all family was looked upon as an outstanding sacrifice. It was described as *peregrinatio pro Dei amore* (pilgrimage for the love of God), *propter nomen Domini* (in the name of the Lord), *pro amore* (for love), *pro Christo* (for Christ), *pro remedio animae* (for the salvation of souls), *pro eterna patria* (for the eternal homeland).[19]

The Inner Pilgrimage

Clearly the contrast between voluntary exile and a strong attachment to place implies the existence of a vision that extended beyond an intimate local landscape to encompass the whole world. Patrick, in one of his authentic texts, mentions being in exile until death. Yet it seems likely that the biblical, Abrahamic, example was a more powerful influence on the very scripture-minded Celtic monastics than that of Patrick.[20]

It is clear from Celtic monastic writings that true pilgrimage was more than simply a physical movement or wandering. There were those people who simply had a wanderlust. They left their country 'in body only' but their spirit was not truly converted.

On the other hand, there were those who left their home 'in zeal of heart though not in body' because of legitimate commitments or ecclesiastical obedience. These pilgrims by desire were seen as people of spiritual virtue. The most perfect pilgrimage, however, was to leave home 'altogether in body and soul'.[21]

The perfect pilgrimage involved an inner as well as an outer change. By leaving the religious settlement and home country, the ascetic also left his or her 'place in the world', that is, status. Beyond the normal boundaries of religious and social life there was no recognised position and therefore no protection. To be an exile was effectively to be outside social structures and independent of ecclesiastical ones.

Here there is a deep connection with the monastic ideal of 'spiritual poverty'. The wanderers witnessed to the radical equality of all people before God. They made themselves displaced persons. Some Celts at least may have been influenced by the concept of *peregrinus* in Roman Law which meant a stranger or a stateless person. God alone became their country of origin and faithfulness to God was what gave them status. This was powerfully expressed by travelling not only to where they were not known, 'nobodies', but where they did not even understand the language.[22]

The pilgrim was a *hospes mundi*, a guest of the world. The great monastic wanderer Columbanus preached the essential instability and transitory nature of earthly life. Life is a roadway which the Christian must travel in perpetual pilgrimage. 'Therefore let this principle abide with us, that on the road we so live as travellers, as pilgrims, as guests of the world [*ut hospites mundi*].'[23] Hagiographical literature reinforced this same spirit of urgency. Here there was no abiding city. So, 'leave thy fatherland for my sake, and get thee out'. Or, 'this is not the place of thy resurrection' – that is, both the particular place where the ascetic was called to abide in expectation of death and the divinely designated entry point into the world of eternity.[24]

If the journey was not well-planned in advance this was because there was, strictly speaking, no temporal destination. So, you set out entrusting yourself to the Lord of the world and the elements. As the Anglo-Saxon Chronicle for 891 records, three Irishmen arrived in Cornwall in a curragh without a steering oar 'because they wanted to go into exile for the love of God, they cared not whither'.[25]

Journey and Mission
There has been a certain amount of debate concerning whether the Celtic *peregrini* can be considered as missionaries. In one sense, the primary motive was spiritual or ascetical. This becomes clear when reading the sermons of Columbanus for example. Yet, characteristically the exiles responded to the interest in Christianity among their new neighbours. The greater personal freedom gained through spiritual pilgrimage also created an ability to adapt easily to local needs. Columbanus and his followers evangelised, and sought Church renewal, across Europe as far south as Italy. In one of his letters to his followers, Columbanus indicates that 'You know I love the salvation of many and seclusion for myself, the one for the progress of the Lord, that is, of His Church, the other for my own desire'. Bede's *Ecclesiastical History* records that Fursa (or Fursey) in East Anglia came 'to spend his life as a pilgrim for the love of our Lord' but 'on his arrival . . . preached the Gospel as he always did'. However, some authorities have described the Celtic Church as a *mission* Church rather than a missionary one. By this they mean that the wandering ascetics did little proactive conversion work outside Britain but, like Columbanus, founded influential spiritual centres across western Europe in countries that were at least nominally Christian.[26]

Changing Attitudes
Although exile and pilgrimage were important features of Celtic spirituality, it is not the case that everyone approved of the trend. There was also some active opposition. Authority conflicts are hinted at even in Adomnan's *Life of Columba*. The holy man Cormac who diligently sought a desert in the ocean failed because he had with him a companion who had departed without his abbot's consent.[27]

It would hardly be surprising that an ascetical practice such as pilgrimage was hotly debated precisely because it contradicted established ecclesiastical and social norms. By conflicting with ordinary monastic existence, exile may have been perceived as undermining the value of settled monastic life. Perhaps it may even have affected the stability of existing settlement patterns? As early as 428, a letter of Pope Celestine, *Cuperemus Quidem*, condemned the practice of appointing *peregrini et extranei* (pilgrims and strangers) to ecclesiastical office over the heads of local, stable, familiar clergy.[28]

By the eighth century, attitudes were changing more broadly even within the Celtic part of the Church. From the mid-700s there was a stream of measures aimed at controlling the activities of the pilgrim ascetics. They were increasingly seen as irresponsible or undesirable. The freedom of the sixth- and seventh-century saints who seem to have been driven onwards in perpetual pilgrimage by an inner prompting did not fit into a more organised Church life. As this emerged, even in its Celtic form, the virtue of stability was increasingly valued. So, monastic reformers advocated a more controlled life. The Rule of Ailbe, for example, enjoined monastics not to desert their communities.[29]

Perhaps part of the reason for the shift of attitude was that the nature of pilgrim journeys had itself altered. The old-style ascetic conception of exile had given way to the world of the ambitious scholar who travelled overseas with a definite end in view. From the ninth century onwards the original attitude to pilgrimage found its clearest expression in some of the poetry of hermits who, paradoxically, did not travel physically at all. So 'pilgrimage' took place increasingly within the cell. The new generation of stable solitaries were the spiritual heirs of the *peregrini*.

> Alone in my little hut without a human being in my company, dear has been the pilgrimage before going to meet death.[30]

The true object of pilgrimage had always been a loving attention to God. Even in the heyday of the wanderers there had been a deep suspicion of pilgrims who did not already carry with them the God whom they sought on their journey.

> Coming to Rome, much labour and little profit! The King whom you seek here, unless you bring Him with you you will not find Him.[31]

Conclusion

As scholars are now realising, the history of spiritual pilgrimage for Christ was not a simple tale of hardy (and perhaps anti-social) ascetics fleeing to windy crags in inhospitable lands. The Celtic wanderers, while deliberately leaving the security of familiar social and religious contexts, took their culture with them. 'Wherever they went, Irish monks took their well-developed social models and their intense need to form communities with them.'[32] Like Columbanus in his journeys across western Europe, most of the exiles left their kin and settlements only to make new sets of relationships and to build new sacred enclosures.

At a certain time, the Celtic wanderers fitted conveniently into the needs of the Church in western Europe. The fifth and sixth centuries were ripe for the plantation of centres of evangelisation or spiritual renewal. The Celtic ascetics could go anywhere. They did not need complex structures of external stability for their life-style or the architecture of decent cloisters and churches. They and their spirituality of journey may have been relatively disorganised. However, a spirituality of journeying makes for a greater flexibility and an ability to rely on the inspiration and enterprise of individuals or small groups. All this was excellently suited to the needs of the times. As a result, the Celtic wanderers were immensely influential not only in the British Isles but also in Gaul, Italy and Germany.[33] Given the fluidity of contemporary western culture, a similar flexibility and mobility may need to characterise the spirituality of our own times.

SIX

The Natural World

Apart from the practice of wandering pilgrimage, another aspect of the spirituality of Celtic Christianity that has received attention in modern studies is its reputed sensitivity to the natural world, including animals. This has led some writers to speak of Celtic spirituality as 'green' or 'ecological' and even to draw parallels with the spirituality of Francis of Assisi.[1] In support of this view the favoured texts are often lyrical nature poems stemming from a hermit movement from the seventh century onwards, although the classic lives of saints suggest intimate relationships with animals.[2] There are also some striking prayers and hymns in the *Carmina Gadelica*, the collection of texts that originate in the oral traditions of the Highlands and western islands of Scotland.[3]

It is certainly true that many of the writings of the Celtic Christian tradition emphasise the immanence of God within the natural world. This awareness of the spiritual dimension of life, and particularly God, in and through nature once again emphasises how 'placed' Celtic Christianity appears to be. A great deal more work needs to be done on the understanding of nature in the broader Christian spiritual tradition. However, there seems to be a case for contrasting Celtic attitudes, at least to some degree, with many other traditional forms of Christianity. All too frequently, the material world was simply a place to be left behind in favour of life on a better, more spiritual plane.

Celtic Christians seem to have inherited much of this emphasis on nature from the religion of their pre-Christian forebears. In fact, the particular sense of the divine presence in all things may have been one of the most important inheritances from 'the old ways'. Traditional Celtic mythology had been fundamentally positive in its understanding of the world. This was because it lacked a sense of human sin and divine punishment. The old gods were beautiful and the Land of Promise had few monsters, no lasting strife, no extremes of climate and very little that was ugly.[4]

Another significant feature was the close connection that was believed to exist between the 'good' ruler and the fertility of the land. Kingship and kinship were fundamental to the Celtic experience and even in the Christian era, for example in the inauguration of the King of Connaught in 1310, there remained elements of the almost mystical union of the king with the land. The king was believed to be 'married' to his land and from this union it was hoped would spring a rich produce. The king must be accepted by the land which would then show its pleasure in his good rule by its fertility.[5]

I do not wish to undermine entirely this modern perception that Celtic Christians had a particular love affair with the natural world, their place in it and the reality of God to be found there. However, there are some qualifications that need to be underlined. First, we must avoid an anachronistic comparison between our contemporary *anxious* approaches to nature and those of an earlier age. Neither the Irish Celtic hermits of the eighth century nor the nineteenth-century Hebridean islanders of Carmichael's collections were concerned *about* nature in our modern sense. Such an attitude in fact represents our collective distancing from the natural world, abuse of it through unreflective use of industrial and technological power, and our subsequent concern to repair the damage through an appropriate ecological consciousness and response. In contrast the Celts, whom we tend to romanticise, simply *lived with* nature because they existed in constant contact with it and could not afford to be disrespectful to it.

I have just said that the Celts *lived with* nature. What is important about this idea is that living with nature can never be a matter of romanticism. The wildness of headlands and the roar of the ocean may stir the blood and the imagination but they also have their physical inconveniences and, indeed, their dangers. Saint Columba of Iona is recorded as warning Brother

Berach of the dangers of the ocean before he set out for a trip to Tiree.

> The saint looked upon him and said: 'My son, be very careful not to attempt to take the direct route across the open sea to the land of Eth [Tiree] this day, but instead to sail around about, by the small islands; lest you be terrified by a prodigious monster, and be scarcely able to escape.'[6]

The Celtic Christians were like any other people of the early medieval period in that they believed that natural forces could both help them and harm them. Medieval Celts thought of themselves in the same categories as the rest of the created world rather than as distinct or isolated from it. They took for granted the fundamental unity and organic connection of nature and human life. The best way to describe this view of world was 'participation in the cosmos'. Consequently, people sought to influence the natural forces within which they existed in ways that were advantageous.[7]

Popular magic in the early Middle Ages was an important means of controlling the world of the spiritual or supernatural powers that surrounded human beings. Sometimes the behaviour and attitudes of Celtic Christians seem to have remained shamelessly magical. This has led later Christians to view Celtic spirituality with great suspicion. In pre-Christian systems of magical thought, nature was not opposed to humankind or perceived as alien. Nature was all-embracing, permeated with powerful forces, and human beings were included in it. Human interaction with the rest of nature was so complete that people were, in a sense, unable to look at it from outside. They would have felt themselves to be imbedded in the power of the cosmos and therefore sought to follow its eternal rhythm. This is why it was necessary to hold feasts and to perform rituals for the continuation of the natural order.

However, there is in fact a significant difference between the Christian religion of the Celts and the purity of their 'old' magic. The difference was that the forces of nature were gradually personified as angels, saints and demons – and even as the

72

mediated presence of the divine. In the Christian image of the world, an almost unconscious unity between humanity and the rest of nature changed into a strained relationship of connected but opposite poles. Humanity and nature were not identical any more. People still felt themselves to be part of nature but at the same time realised their alienation from it. The link between was no longer organic but symbolic.

The famous protection prayer already cited from the monastic Rule of Tallaght involved signing a blessing to all four quarters of the world as well as earth and heaven. This is probably adapted from pre-Christian sources. Whatever the changes in attitude to nature brought about by Christianity, this reminds us that the Celtic Christians had few romantic notions but were well aware of the potential instability of the physical world around them.[8]

The Celtic Christian attitude to nature involved a profound sense of the immanence of God. This reminds us that it was not nature *as such* that concerned the Celts. Nature was a kind of second sacred book, parallel to the scriptures, that revealed the divine. Did the contemplative Celtic ascetics really notice the natural world in our sense of a beautiful landscape? This is difficult to assess but nature itself was not the object of contemplation. Although there was an immediacy in the way a human relationship with nature was expressed, for example in some early medieval Irish poetry, nature was not really a value in itself. What the monastic poets sought and found in the natural world was an image of the creator-God.

It is interesting that there is certainly a close connection between the vivid Irish poetic response to the natural world and the ascetic reforms of the hermit movement. Although some scholars think that nature poetry, especially that linked to the seasons, had remote connections to a pre-Christian past, most would agree that the bulk of 'nature poems' belong to the religious revival of the eighth and ninth centuries. Ascetics retired from normal settlements to find solitude, surrounded by the sights and sound of the sea or of the woods. Their imagination was quickened to observe the natural world with a new awareness. Even if we are to say that a spiritual horizon was uppermost, the anonymous monastic poets also had an exquisite delight in the variety of life around them.[9]

Yet, once again, even in those situations where Celtic ascetics obviously admired certain sites, the natural as such was only a relative value. It was the spiritual quality of a place that really counted. It is no coincidence that what was seen as 'beautiful' in Celtic religious poetry was often simplicity, wildness and the solitude of particular locations. One well-known anonymous ninth-century poem expresses the mixture of sentiments particularly well.

> I wish, O son of the Living God,
> O ancient, eternal King,
> For a hidden little hut in the wilderness
> That it may be my dwelling.
>
> An all-grey lithe little lark
> To be by its side,
> A clear pool to wash away sins
> Through the grace of the Holy Spirit.
>
> Quite near, a beautiful wood,
> Around it on every side,
> To nurse many-voiced birds,
> Hiding it with its shelter.
>
> And facing the south for warmth;
> A little brook across its floor,
> A choice ground with many gracious gifts
> Such as which be good for every plant....
>
> A pleasant church and with the linen altar-cloth,
> A dwelling for God from Heaven;
> Then, shining candles
> Above the pure white Scriptures....
>
> This is the husbandry I would take,
> I would choose, and will not hide it:
> Fragrant leek,
> Hens, salmon, trout, bees.

Raiment and food enough for me
From the King of fair fame,
And I to be sitting for a while
Praying God in every place.[10]

The Irish monastic tradition produced in one of its saints, Kevin, a figure whose legend in some ways bears comparison with those surrounding Francis of Assisi. Kevin settled in the beautiful solitude of Glendalough in County Wicklow. It was said of him that he cultivated the friendship of beasts and birds. A friendly badger brought him a daily salmon to eat and once rescued his prayer book when it had fallen into a lake. Flocks of birds sang round about him as he prayed. On one occasion, when a blackbird had built a nest on his outstretched palms, he was said to have kept the prayerful posture until the babies were hatched! While what is immediately attractive is the natural imagery, it is important to remember that such tales of wild animals being in harmony with monks and ascetics were quite conventional in monastic hagiography, East and West. The tales were themselves images of a return to the unfallen state of the Garden of Eden. In other words, it is the virtues of monastic life rather than nature itself that lie at the heart of such stories.

This emphasis on hermitages or monastic enclosures as re-creations of a new Eden also implied that the presence of God was not to be experienced merely in a future life but could be enjoyed now, even if only in a transitory way. The natural world became, therefore, a favoured image of theophany. One hermit poet looked out over the sea from his island cell, listening to the waves breaking on the rocks and to the gull's cry, while watching the smooth strand by the headland, the flocks of birds, the mighty whales. And all the while he blessed the Lord 'who has power over all'. Another hermit exclaimed that we should adore the Lord who is maker of 'the white-waved sea on earth'.[11]

The dual themes of the closeness of heaven and harmony with nature overlapped when the Archangel Michael appeared to Brendan during his famous voyage in the form of a bird singing sweet music. The Irish monk Ciaran's first disciples were a bear,

75

a fox, a badger, a wolf and a hind who not only could live with him but, equally extraordinarily, with each other.[12]

In the end, as one of Columbanus' sermons reminds us, it was of course not particular, especially beautiful places but the whole of the natural order that was filled with the divine presence and power.

> Yet of His being who shall be able to speak? Of how He is everywhere present and invisible, or of how He fills heaven and earth and every creature, according to that saying, Do I not fill heaven and earth? saith the Lord, and elsewhere, The Spirit of God, according to the prophet, has filled the round earth, and again, Heaven is my throne, but earth is the footstool of my feet?

The 'incarnation', as it were, of God in nature is, for Columbanus, significant in two ways. First, it indicates unequivocally the closeness of God to us.

> Therefore God is everywhere, utterly vast, and everywhere nigh at hand, according to His own witness of Himself; I am, He says, a God at hand and not a God afar off.

Secondly, nature is like a second revelation, a 'book' to be 'read' alongside the scriptures as we seek to deepen our knowledge of who God is.

> Seek no farther concerning God; for those who wish to know the great deep must first review the natural world. For knowledge of the Trinity is properly likened to the depths of the sea, according to that saying of the Sage, And the great deep, who shall find it out? If then a man wishes to know the deepest ocean of divine understanding, let him first if he is able scan that visible sea, and the less he finds himself to understand of those creatures which lurk beneath the waves, the more let him realize that he can know less of the depths of its Creator.[13]

A second popular source these days for the Celtic view of the natural world comes from the oral tradition of hymns, prayers, incantations and blessings that were collected in the Highlands and islands of Scotland by the nineteenth-century civil servant, Alexander Carmichael. In recent years a number of scholars have questioned how much of the material is authentic and how much the product of Carmichael's fertile imagination. More recently, John MacInnes' detailed preface to a new edition of *Carmina Gadelica*, while by no means naive about the critical issues, effectively rehabilitates the majority of the material as reasonably authentic.[14]

On the face of it, the context of Carmichael's collection seems a long way from the ascetical hermit cells of the ninth century. Carmichael's sources were crofters and fisherfolk, predominantly but not exclusively Roman Catholics. He thought rather romantically that the origins of the material lay centuries back in the monastic settlements of Derry or Iona. We may accept that the connections forged by oral tradition may easily stretch from the 1860s back to the first half of the seventeenth century. However, it would be to push matters beyond the evidence to make direct connections to the old monastic traditions. What probably connects the two great sources of Celtic 'nature literature' is a more general cultural 'sensitivity', a shared island geography and a pre-industrial life-style of fishing and farming close to the natural rhythm of the seasons.

In reflecting on Celtic nature writing, it seems valid to make a distinction between lauding the inherently spiritual qualities *of* nature and reflecting on the spiritual presence incarnated *in* or revealed *through* nature. If we accept that distinction, it is easier to say that Celtic Christianity had a very high view of nature in the second sense. There are a number of common characteristics to this.

First, creation is good and God is to be experienced in the natural world. This leads to an intimate affection for nature as 'revelation'.

> Delightful I think it to be in the bosom of an isle, on the peak of a rock, that I might often see there the calm of the sea.
>
> That I might see its heavy waves over the glittering ocean, as they chant a melody to their Father on their eternal course.[15]

The natural world itself also has the power to 'recognise' the sacred and the holy. The Irish ascetic Mael Anfaidh saw a little bird wailing and sorrowing and wondered why. An angel appeared to explain.

> 'Well now, priest,' said the angel, 'let it not trouble you any more. Mo Lua son of Ocha has died, and that is why the living things bewail him, for he never killed a living thing, great or small; not more do men bewail him that the other living things do, and among them the little bird that you see.'[16]

The famous hymn, the Lorica or St Patrick's Breastplate (in fact composed no earlier than the eighth century), links the power and presence of God to the world of creation:

> I gird myself today with the
>   might of heaven:
> The rays of the sun,
> The beams of the moon,
> The glory of fire,
> The speed of wind,
> The depth of sea,
> The stability of earth,
> The hardness of rock.[17]

Similar sentiments are expressed in the wonderful prayer recorded in Carmichael's *Carmina Gadelica* that speaks of the presence of God in and through the gifts of nature:

> There is no plant in the ground
> But is full of His virtue,
> There is no form in the strand
> But is full of His blessing.
>
> There is no bird on the wing,
> There is no star in the sky,
> There is nothing beneath the sun,
> But proclaims His goodness.[18]

To borrow a phrase from the fourteenth-century English mystic Julian of Norwich, God's reality for Celtic Christians was 'homely'. The divine presence was something immediate and intimate rather than distant. An anonymous ninth-century Irish author could write unashamedly in the language of intimacy and, at the same time, express the sense of God's presence and action in the natural world. 'My darling, God of heaven, was the thatcher who has thatched it'.[19] Another text, this time from the Scottish *Carmina Gadelica*, expresses not only a strongly Christocentric theology of re-creation but also suggests that the natural world was important precisely as revelatory rather than purely on its own terms.

> A time ere came the Son of God,
>   The earth was a black morass,
> Without star, without sun, without moon,
>   Without body, without heart, without form.
>
> Illumined plains, illumined hills,
>   Illumined the great green sea,
> Illumined the whole globe together,
>   When the Son of God came to earth.[20]

However, it was not merely the incarnate Christ who was felt to be close at hand but also the Trinity. This is beautifully expressed in a baptism-related blessing prayer for a new child recited by Hebridean midwives:

> The little drop of the Father
>   On thy little forehead, beloved one.
>
> The little drop of the Son,
>   On thy little forehead, beloved one.
>
> The little drop of the Spirit
>   On thy little forehead, beloved one.[21]

For many western Christians the Trinity is scarcely an object of devotion even if the person of Jesus Christ is. Yet, for many Celtic Christians it was the presence of the Trinity that was powerfully felt.

> The Three Who are over me,
> The Three Who are below me,
> The Three Who are above me here,

> The Three Who are above me yonder;
> The Three Who are in the earth,
> The Three Who are in the air,
> The Three Who are in the heaven,
>   The Three Who are in the great pouring sea.[22]

This sense of closeness to a God who is the one-in-three, a community of persons in a harmonious and equal unity, probably reflects the strong sense of family, household and kin in Celtic society.

This brings us to a second major characteristic of the Celtic Christian approach to the world. That is, there was no real divide between this world and the 'other' world of divine and spiritual beings. God was close at hand, but so were the saints and the angels. The nearness of God to creation went hand in hand with a sense of the heavenly powers surrounding people day and night. It seemed natural to Celtic Christians to turn not only to God but to angels and saints for support. This included practical assistance in even the most mundane things such as getting dressed, lighting a fire and milking a cow. The Blessing of the Kindling begins:

> I will kindle my fire this morning
> In presence of the holy angels of heaven,[23]

A simple phrase such as the Scottish 'Bless the handling of my hands' expresses a deep desire to consecrate to God all that is done in the day. Prayer grew out of daily rhythms of the Celtic way of life.

> Bless, O God, my little cow,
>   Bless, O God, my desire;
> Bless Thou my partnership
>   And the milking of my hands, O God.[24]

Angels play a striking role in Celtic spirituality. This is especially true of the Archangel Michael whose feast day was one of the great events in Scottish islands right up until the mid-nineteenth century.

> Be the red-white Michael meeting the soul,

80

Early and late, night and day,
Early and late, night and day.[25]

To understand Celtic Christianity fully we have to come to terms with this perhaps unfamiliar sense of the nearness and perceptible nature of the 'other world'. What was normally invisible could break through into human perception. The invocation of saints or angels was not a matter of calling down strange powers from outside human experience. Rather it concerned a bringing into explicit consciousness a dimension of the created world. The existence of the Communion of Saints that Christians affirm in the Creed was a very strong experience. The blessed dead were in some sense already risen yet still part of the Church and therefore living presences among the human community on earth.[26]

Unless we are hopelessly romantic we cannot ignore the fact that Celtic Christian spirituality also has a rather unattractive and extreme ascetic streak. The point is, however, that this is somehow balanced by the fact that the Celts also took very seriously that we can and should enjoy the things of God. The most tangible gift is the created world around us. Celtic spirituality in the end steers a kind of middle way between extreme asceticism and extreme sensuality. The key to this balance is a deep sense of unity and harmony – within the individual person and between people and the surrounding world. This sense is caught in the words from a Scottish prayer, 'O bless myself entire'.

I have already indicated the importance for Celtic religion of 'edges' or boundaries of all kinds. These edges connect the solid and material with the intangible, the seen with the unseen, this world with another world (of God, saints, angels and the dead) which is always alongside us. The understanding of nature in Celtic spirituality arises from a sense of living within a 'cosmos of the edge'. Human places, natural features and landscapes are at the same time the concrete world of our daily experience in which we consciously live and yet something more. They also constitute a world of wonder, power, spirits and God. This is why it was so important in Celtic religious sensibility and behaviour to feel that the relationship between earthly and divine realities was correctly maintained.

In the fourth stanza of St Patrick's Breastplate the rocks and the sea are actually invoked as spiritual powers: 'For my shield this day I call . . . Ocean's depth, Earth's solidity, Rock's immobility'. This may be thought by some to be close to animism! Perhaps the Celtic Christian view of the natural world does at times walk something of a tightrope. My sense, however, is that something quite subtle and important is being maintained. God's indwelling Spirit is not merely in humankind or even in animate objects. The Spirit dwells in all things without exception. In that sense the elements such as earth and water are powerful spiritual forces because they have within them the creative energy that is God's own.

Iona: Place and Pilgrimage

The island of Iona is offshore from the larger island of Mull on the west coast of Scotland. Early medieval pilgrims to the island undoubtedly knew a great deal more about hardship and discomfort than any modern traveller. However, even nowadays the journey to the island is long, quite complicated and even relatively uncomfortable for the city-dweller who is used to the smooth and speedy simplicity of most modern journeys. A recent journey from London involved me in five and a half hours on a train, a taxi ride across Glasgow, another three hours by train to Oban, an overnight stop, the early ferry to the Isle of Mull, a long bus ride across the island and finally another ferry! Iona is a place you must *want* to visit. It is not a minor detour for the casual visitor.

What do pilgrims, medieval or modern, discover on landing on the Isle of Iona? Topographically, it is a small and relatively insignificant place – only about three-and-a-half miles long by one-and-a-half miles wide. Its highest point, Dun I, rises no more than about 350 feet above sea level. Even Adomnan, the hagiographer of Iona's great monastic founder Columba, described Iona as 'this small and remote island of the Britannic ocean'.[1] Despite the importance for the spread of Christianity in the British Isles of Columba and the monastic family he created, Adomnan obviously did not harbour any illusions that Iona was the centre of the universe.

Yet, Iona has had a remarkable history that makes some reflection on it in relation to the themes we have explored an apt landing place after our brief voyage through the Celtic seas. The community Columba founded there was not only the direct ancestor of much of the Christian Church in Scotland; through its daughter settlement on the island of Lindisfarne (or Holy Island) Iona was also indirectly the source of Christianity in northern England. It seems possible that Iona may have been

83

the place of origin of the famous Book of Kells with its striking examples of Celtic Christian design. The island has a remarkably continuous religious history and significance. This stretches from pre-Christian times via the Celtic monastic settlement and its Benedictine and Augustinian successors down to the modern Iona Community and the restoration of the medieval abbey buildings in the twentieth century. There is an equally long tradition of pilgrimage to 'the place of Columba'. This is evidenced by, for example, the cairns of stones on the beach of St Columba's Bay that may have been constructed by medieval pilgrims as devotional acts.

What gives Iona its special quality is probably a mixture of this sense of history, of a humanly and spiritually significant place in the landscape, with the striking effects of the light, the wildness of the elements and the natural beauty. The late George MacLeod, founder of the modern Iona Community and rebuilder of the abbey church, is said to have described Iona as 'a thin place' – a place where the membrane between the material world and the world of spiritual realities is particularly thin.

Continuities in Time and Place

We have seen that continuities of place and life were important in Celtic spiritual sensibilities. As with so many Celtic sites, Iona intertwines the two apparently conflicting forces of pre-Christian and Christian religious symbolism and practice. Despite popular legend and the peculiar certainties of modern New Age pilgrims, there is no clear evidence that Iona was a special religious centre for druid worship and there is no identifiable druid site. True, the Coronation Stone at Westminster Abbey is said to have druidic associations and to be one of the so-called Iona Black Stones. These stones were apparently sited quite near the abbey and the last of them disappeared in the nineteenth century. It is also recorded that at one time Iona was called 'The Druids' Island' and that there had been a circle of standing stones. Such traditions cannot be rejected entirely and some or all of the stories may be true. Nevertheless there is no hard evidence to support the claims.[2]

However, there seem to be more reliable religious continuities. Near to the centre of the island is a large mound called 'Hill of the Angels' (*Cnoc nan Aingeal*). This has strong associations with both pre-Christian and Christian religion. The legend surrounding its name is that Columba was once seen there by other monks surrounded by angels while in deep prayer. But it is also known that the hill is associated with pre-Christian spirits and rituals. Whether St Columba prayed there, or his mystical experience became fused with older, spiritual presences, or there was simply an association of two things in people's memories, the continuity is still there and recalled in the name.

Even into early modern times, the islanders brought horses to circle the hill on the Eve of St Michael's Day in late September. Commentators have noted that the turn was made sun-wise. So, in one of those typical Celtic examples of the elision of pre-Christian custom with Christian belief, the good Presbyterian islanders were unwittingly dedicating their horses to the sun god! In addition, until the end of the eighteenth century the ancient tradition of Great Gruel Thursday was enacted on the western shore at midnight before Maundy Thursday. In an offering to the sea (originally the god Shony) someone waded into the waves to pour out gruel or ale in the hope that the sea would provide a plentiful supply of seaweed to fertilise the second ploughing of spring.[3]

Other pre-Christian practices survived, or re-emerged after the Reformation. The former sacred places, such as the abbey church, were plundered for trinkets. Although by the end of the seventeenth century the church was ruined, the medieval marble altar is recorded as still standing. Yet, some fifty years later it seems to have been in fragments because the islanders broke off pieces to use for healing purposes.[4]

Of course one of the other great examples of spiritual continuity on Iona was the way that the medieval Benedictine foundation sought to align itself physically on the Columban site. One of the obvious intentions of the religious modernisers who introduced Roman styles of monastic community to Scotland was to place an abbey on Iona precisely so that the Benedictines would inherit Columba's reputation. Dates are imprecise but the *Annals of Ulster* suggest that traditional Celtic monastic life survived on Iona as late as 1164 and the Benedictine Abbey was founded somewhere around 1200. There is a possibility, therefore, that a still existing Celtic community (or part of it) was simply absorbed into the new ways.[5]

The location of the Benedictine buildings appears to have been on the foundations of the Celtic structures and adjacent to Columba's shrine. There is only one building, however, that seems to date back to the Celtic period. That is the mainly twelfth-century St Oran's Chapel next to the cemetery and to the south-west of the abbey complex at the end of the medieval paved roadway known as 'the road of the dead'. Unusually for an abbey in cold northern climes, the cloister and living quarters were built on the *north* side of the church rather than on the relatively sunny south side. Looked at from one perspective, this fact was governed by the position of water sources needed for sanitation. However, the church could have been built to the north of the stream thus preserving the normal southern position for living quarters. The only reason for the chosen layout can have been the desire for continuity in the site of the Columban church and shrine.[6]

Religion in the Landscape

Ireland, Scotland and Northumbria belonged for a long time to one cultural area. In this context, the central position of Iona means that the island was probably quite important in facilitating communications despite its small size. The same factor that made Iona such a good site for communication rebounded on it when the sea-routes were threatened by Viking sea power. The murder of monks on the island on several occasions at the hands of Vikings is recorded in the two place names of 'Martyrs' Bay' and 'White Strand of the Monks'.[7]

Iona was typical of many Celtic religious settlements in that it was both remote and accessible. It was remote in the sense that it was an island with no really satisfactory harbour and whose sea approaches were hazardous. However, from the land

side it was less than a mile from Mull and most of the wood
and some of the stone that was needed for the monastery buildings were shipped across the sound. There are many records of
the monks being sailors and the great burial ground near the
present abbey seems to have attracted the great and good from
other islands and from the mainland of Scotland.[8]

Although the stories associated with Columba seem to point
to the accidental quality of his arrival there, it is likely that his
'pilgrimage' involved an awareness of the island's potential as a
sanctuary for him and his followers. The island seems to have
been well known and there may have been an element of plan-
ning in the landing. Certainly the island proved feasible as a
religious settlement for very practical reasons. The earth was
sufficiently fertile to raise crops. The eastern shore was protected
from Atlantic storms by a low ridge of hills. There were plenty
of streams for drinking water and sanitation. Most important of
all there was an adequate portion of flat land for settling a
community on the protected side which also gave access to the
narrow sound across to Mull.[9]

Like so many Celtic sacred sites, Iona even today is full of
legends associated with particular physical features. There is the
Hill of the Angels already mentioned. There is also the Hill of
the Seat at the north end where Columba is supposed to have
sat meditating. At the south end, to the west of Columba's Bay,
there is the Cairn of the Back to Ireland where Columba is
reputed to have climbed on arrival on Iona to check whether he
could still see the coast of Ulster before burying his coracle.[10]
Every part of the island has a story. Inlets, beaches and hills
have names that are descriptive of people or events. There is a
typical Celtic delight in immortalising small details of history
by naming places, even physically insignificant ones, after them.
Such local, even domestic, events would probably otherwise
have been forgotten. Celtic places remain, as it were, inhabited
by a past that is joined to the present by strong threads of story
and naming.

Ordering Sacred Places

On Iona there is surviving evidence of the kind of physical boundary that, as I have already noted, traditionally surrounded Celtic sacred space. In fact the remains of the earth *vallum* or rampart to the north and west of the present abbey are the only evidence above ground of the original Celtic religious settlement. The remaining line of the rampart has been traced. It is not a sacred circle as in some settlements but a rectangle surrounding about twenty acres of land and centred on *Torr an Aba* which is reputedly the site of Columba's cell and therefore specially sacred. Such ramparts were, as we have seen, more than defensive walls. They marked a legal and symbolic boundary for the holy enclosure of the community.

If we scan the pages of Adomnan's *Life* we will find scattered throughout the work some details about how the overall enclosure was divided. There was a church with an attached chamber, a number of working or sleeping huts for the monks, the hut where Columba 'all night... used to have for bed the bare rock; and for pillow, a stone which even today stands beside his burial-place as a kind of grave-pillar'.[11] There was another hut on a higher place used by Columba for writing, a guest house, a communal building. All of these surrounded an open space.

One interesting item that we can draw from Adomnan's descriptions was that Columba had a separate cell. This would follow the Celtic practice of having some ascetics who lived a hermit life within the wider enclosure. In the middle of the island even today there is *Cobhan Cuilteach*, 'the remote hollow', where there are the stone foundations of a small hut. The dating of the ruins is uncertain and the popular title 'Culdee's Cell' is a mistranslation of the Gaelic. However, it is generally accepted that this is the remains of a hermit cell probably in the form of a traditional beehive hut. If so, it once again fits the overall pattern of Celtic religious life where some ascetics retired to a deeper solitude away from the general enclosure. *The Irish Life of Adamnan*[12] notes that there were such distinctions within the monastic community on Iona. Some monks led a more contemplative life and others conducted some kind of

88

active ministry. However, all the monks did manual labour without distinction.

The *Irish Life* also suggests that there was a nuns' enclosure on the island. It refers to a priest friend of Columba dying near to the enclosure and the nuns coming out to give assistance. The question as to whether there were indeed women on Columba's Iona at all, let alone within the sacred enclosure, is interesting and the evidence is controversial. The presence of a small island between Iona and Mull called *Eilean nam Ban*, 'the women's island', is a reminder of one tradition that Columba banished all women and cows from Iona! This seems very unlikely. Apart from the reference to nuns in the *Irish Life*, there are other hints of women on Iona. So, for example, there exists a story of Columba conversing with an old woman in the cemetery as she cut nettles to make a broth for herself.[13]

It is just possible that *Eilean nam Ban* was where the *manaig*, or married monks, lived. As we have seen, such people were common in Celtic monastic communities. However, it was also common for them to live in a distinct area and only to enter the deepest part of the sacred enclosure to worship in church or in times of danger.

On Iona during the Middle Ages a memory that traditional Celtic monasticism was far from exclusively celibate may have persisted, at least unconsciously. Certainly the practice of monastic concubinage was remarkably widespread in Celtic areas even after traditional communities had been replaced by Roman styles of monasticism inspired by the Rule of St Benedict for example. Several monks of Iona Abbey, including its abbots, were recorded as having partners and children during the High Middle Ages. One of them called Dominic, who was a monk at the turn of the fifteenth century, was father of three children who became respectively the parish priest of Iona, a monk at the abbey and an Augustinian canoness at the island convent.[14]

Marking the Boundaries
If cemeteries and High Crosses are to be considered the most obvious boundary markers significant to the Celtic tradition,

Iona is particularly well blessed. It was common for monastic and other religious enclosures to centre on the tomb of the saintly founder who remained the focus for his often scattered 'family' or spiritual kin. In the case of Iona this is obviously Columba. St Columba's Shrine is the name given to a small chapel that is sited at the entrance of the abbey church, to the north of the great west door. It seems that this chapel was originally free-standing. The site probably dates back to the ninth century although the present structure is largely a recent restoration. There is evidence of burials beneath the floor but these seem to be medieval. However, the tradition that this is the site of Columba's grave and shrine is still thought by scholars to be possible. Certainly, the positioning of the High Crosses nearby would indicate that it was a site of some importance.

Iona possesses the remains of no less than five ancient High Crosses (not to mention the later medieval MacLean's Cross near the parish church). Only one of these, St Martin's Cross, is complete and standing on its original site near the west front of the present abbey church. Grouped with it is the stump of St Matthew's Cross and the modern replica of the great St John's Cross. The artistically important remains of the original St John's Cross (now in pieces), along with the remains of two other crosses from the Reilig Odhrain graveyard, are in the abbey museum.

Such a cluster of three High Crosses was clearly intended to mark a very significant sacred place – probably the grave of the founder of the Iona paruchia, Columba, and the site of the ancient church building. Adomnan records that crosses were used to mark sacred places. Thus one was said to mark where Columba's uncle, the priest Ernan, dropped dead and another where Columba himself was standing when this happened.[15]

Pre-Christian and Christian motifs fuse in the symbolism of the Iona crosses as they do with so many Celtic markers of sacred place. On one side of a cross might be a series of biblical scenes while on the reverse might be traditional Celtic spiral patterns and an abundance of nature symbols. On Iona crosses spiral patterns and nature symbols combine into a weaving vine –

perhaps signifying the intertwining of the worlds of earth and spirit. There is also a wonderful combination of Trinitarian motifs with nature symbolism. For example, there is a striking design of three eggs in what is either a basket or a bird's nest. There are particularly good examples of this on the arms of the St John's Cross. It has been suggested that the characteristic ring of Celtic High Crosses originated on Iona and then spread to Ireland. Although there clearly was a symbolic value to the cross rings (or, rather, several layers of symbolism) St John's Cross seems to have been designed originally with no ring and only had one added after a mishap snapped the arms off the cross.[16]

The ancient cemetery of Iona is called *Reilig Odhrain*. It, and the neighbouring St Oran's Chapel, is named after Oran or Odhrain, a cousin of Columba. Whether or not this is the site of the ancient monastic cemetery is unclear. It certainly dates back to the early Christian period. Its importance is marked by the paved remains of a medieval pilgrim walk from the cemetery towards the abbey church – perhaps symbolically marking the passage from death to resurrection.

There are a number of memorial slabs from the early period still surviving as well as effigies commemorating the long tradition of burials of the great Highland families. Ancient legend has it that the Kings of Scotland, Ireland and Norway used to be buried here but, while the story underlines the perceived importance of Iona, there is no real evidence that this is true. There is concrete evidence of the peculiar significance for Celts of burial places as boundaries between the material and spiritual worlds in a custom that was still practised as late as the nineteenth century. People were invited to use a hollow in the remaining cross base near the chapel in order to spin small stones as a way of prediction and luck.[17]

Pilgrimage and Journey
Peregrinatio, or pilgrimage for Christ, may be said to be central to Celtic spirituality. It may also be said that Iona itself was founded on pilgrimage. There seems to be some ambiguity about the motivations of the historical Columba. However, it may well

be that one of the reasons why he chose to pilgrim away from Ulster was the renunciation of wealth and political power as an ascetical action. Because of the all-pervading strength of kinship relations a physical departure overseas may have been the only viable way to bring this about. Columba's destination was unlikely to have been random. Some scholars consider that his royal connections made settlement on Iona possible, half-way between two probable sets of family connections in Ireland and Scotland.[18]

The pilgrim theme is strong in the Columban tradition. The *Irish Life* uses the Genesis story of Abraham, called away by God from his native land to a land of promise, as the powerful basis for Columban spirituality. Later the *Irish Life* explicitly links pilgrimage with preaching the word of God.[19] Adomnan's *Life* also uses the classic language of pilgrimage spirituality to describe Columba. *Pro Christo peregrinari volens enavigavit*, 'he sailed away, wishing to be a pilgrim for Christ'.[20] Columba himself is said at one point to have described himself as having completed thirty years of pilgrimage in Britain.[21] There are references to other pilgrims for Christ such as Cormac 'who sought with great labour not less than three times a desert in the ocean, and yet found none'.[22] And there are a number of other references in Adomnan's story to life itself as a pilgrimage.

The Natural World

Apart from the fact that Iona is a naturally beautiful place, there is not a great deal in the written lives of Columba that points explicitly to a strong affinity with the natural world. There are legends however. On the northern headland of the island there is a small rise called *Cnoc an Suidhe*, 'The Hill of the Seat', where Columba is reputed to have sat to gaze at the wild sea beyond the dazzling white sands of the shoreline. Certainly this particular spot, and the quality of light that gathers there, has appealed to many artists who have visited Iona. In addition, the Celtic hagiographical tradition tends to emphasise the harmony between nature and humanity. Thus, as a matter of fact as well as legend, neither Ireland nor Iona has poisonous beasts or snakes.[23]

All the evidence is that the daily life of Columba and his monks was extremely hard. So they would hardly have had a romantic view of nature. The brothers were out every day cultivating in the face of a variable and harsh climate. Yet, it would also seem that the elements were part of their consciousness. Iona as a whole, rather than the limited enclosure within the ramparts, was seen as 'the monastery'. The *vallum* or enclosure was the ocean and the spiritual mantle was the sky.

It is probably the case that the Book of Kells (now housed in Trinity College, Dublin) was created in part on Iona before being shipped off to Ireland in the face of Viking pillaging and there completed. If so, the great symbolic art of this book may be taken as a summary of Iona's integration of theology and nature. Nature symbolism seems to have been close to the community's heart. The artist(s) of the book provided delightful drawings of cats, cocks, goats, mice and other animals to mingle with intertwining spirals, leaves and foliage in the illuminated text.

Epilogue

Interest in Celtic spirituality, both in its Christian and pre-Christian forms, is experiencing a great revival. Present-day Iona, not least its resident Abbey community, is one of the places that lies at the heart of this movement. It is a place of pilgrimage – nowadays less to visit the shrine of Columba than in search of broadly based spiritual renewal. Of course, that was always the purpose at the heart of every Christian pilgrimage. In the present climate of enthusiasm, we need to remember that the Celtic spiritual sensibility never died out in the British Isles despite the efforts of Latin Christians or Protestants. However, except in remote regions, Celtic spirituality remained largely unknown and out of the mainstream. Those who 'rediscover' it today are often urban people who sense that their spirituality is out of touch with nature, the body and the imagination.

In one sense, the Celtic spirituality that I have described is not simply a rediscovery but a *reinvention*. Those for whom it is truly native soil live within it rather than analyse its significant themes. There is a danger that either we force the history and tradition of particular spiritualities into the shape of other, modern, experiences or we seek to shape our own contemporary spiritual quest naively in terms of some presumed golden age. Despite this, I believe that there can, with care, be a fruitful conversation between our present horizons and those of the great classical spiritual traditions that respects the integrity of both. I am hopeful that the renewed interest in Celtic Christianity will be of this kind.

Notes

INTRODUCTION

1. See my *Spirituality and History: Questions of Interpretation and Method*, London/ New York, 1992, pp.67–69, 124–125.

2. For example, Patrick Thomas, *Candle in the Darkness: Celtic Spirituality from Wales*, Llandysul, Dyfed, 1993.

3. See Charles Thomas, *Celtic Britain*, London, 1986, pp.114–115.

4. See, for example, Diarmuid O Laoghaire, 'Celtic Spirituality' in Cheslyn Jones, Geoffrey Wainwright and Edward Yarnold (eds) *The Study of Spirituality*, London 1986, p.218. Two recent general overviews of Celtic spirituality are, Esther de Waal, *A World Made Whole*, London, 1991, and Ian Bradley, *The Celtic Way*, London, 1993.

5. See, for example, Charles Thomas, p.54.

CHAPTER ONE

1. See Valerie Flint, *The Rise of Magic in Early Medieval Europe*, Oxford, 1991.

2. See T.G.E. Powell, *The Celts*, London, 1980, pp.144–147.

3. See Charles Thomas, pp.123–127.

4. Nora Chadwick, *The Celts*, London, 1971, pp.193–194.

5. Charles Thomas, p.128.

6. Charles Thomas, p.129.

7. J.R. Morris, 'The Literary Evidence' in M.W. Barley and R.P.C. Hanson (eds), *Christianity in Britain 300–700*, Leicester, 1968, p.71.

8. See, for example, Bede, *Ecclesiastical History of the English People*, translated Leo Shirley-Price, London, revised edition 1990, III, 4 & 5, pp.148, 150.

9. James Bulloch, *The Life of the Celtic Church*, Edinburgh, 1963, p.167.

10. See Richard Morris, *Churches in the Landscape*, London, 1989, pp.100–102.

11. Charles Thomas, p.134. Nora Chadwick, *The Age of the Saints in the Early Celtic Church*, London, 1961, pp.51–60, also posits a direct connection between the Celtic Church and the eastern Mediterranean. More recently, see W.H. Frend, 'Ecclesia Britannica: Prelude or Dead End?', in *The Journal of Ecclesiastical History*, 30:2 (April 1979), pp. 129–144.

12. Charles Thomas, p.135. On the early development of the Church in Ireland, see E.G. Bowen, *Saints, Seaways and Settlements*, Cardiff, 1977, Chapter V 'Ireland'.

13. See D. Greene, 'Some Linguistic Evidence Relating to the British Church' in Barley and Hanson, pp.84–85.

14. See Patrick Wormald, 'The Venerable Bede and the "Church of the English" ' in Geoffrey Rowell (ed.), *The English Religious Tradition and the Genius of Anglicanism*, Wantage, 1993, p.16 and n.11.

15. See Richard Sharpe, 'Churches and Communities in early medieval Ireland: towards a pastoral model' in John Blair and Richard Sharpe (eds), *Pastoral Care Before the Parish*, Leicester, 1992, pp.81–109.

16. Morris in Barley and Hanson, p.69.

17. See, for example, Bowen, pp.125–128 and R.P.C. Hanson, 'The Mission of Saint Patrick' in James Mackey (ed.), *An Introduction to Celtic Christianity*, Edinburgh, 1989, especially pp.41–42.

18. Chadwick, *The Celts*, pp.202–203. Kathleen Hughes, *Church and Society in Ireland AD 400–1200*, London, 1987, Section 1, p.20.

19. Bulloch, pp.157–158, 162.

20. Chadwick, *The Age of the Saints*, pp.30–32. A classic, and relatively modern, version of the supposed continuity of the Columban Church in the reformed Church of Scotland is J.A. Duke, *The Columban Church*, Edinburgh, reprinted 1957, cited in Wormald, 'The Venerable Bede', p.13.

21. John T. McNeill, *The Celtic Churches: A History A.D. 200–1200*, Chicago, 1974, p.70.

22. Bulloch, p.168.

23. Kathleen Hughes and Ann Hamlin, *Celtic Monasticism: The Modern Traveller to the Irish Church*, New York, 1981, p.106.

24. Lisa Bitel, *Isle of the Saints: Monastic Settlement and Christian Community in Early Ireland*, Ithaca, New York, 1990, p.242.

25. See Bede, *Ecclesiastical History of the English People*, ed. B. Colgrave and R.A.B. Mynors, Oxford, 1969, Introduction, p.xxv.

26. Hughes and Hamlin, p.30.

27. A classic account is Peter Brown, *The Cult of the Saints*, London/Chicago, 1981. See especially Chapter 1.

28. Powell, *The Celts*, pp.166–167.

29. Richard Morris, p.50.

30. Richard Morris, p.84.

31. Richard Morris, p.56.

32. On the general question of the attitude to pre-Christian religion during the Christian evangelisation of early medieval Europe, see Anton Wessels, *Europe: Was It Ever Really Christian?*, London, English translation 1994, especially Chapter III 'The Celtic Contextualisation'.

33. Bitel, *Isle of the Saints*, p.44.

34. Hughes and Hamlin, p.31.

35. See Powell, *The Celts*, pp.182–184. Also Alwyn and Brinley Rees, *Celtic Heritage: Ancient Tradition in Ireland and Wales*, London, reprint 1990, pp.111, 140ff., 156ff.

36. Pierre Riché, 'Spirituality in Germanic and Celtic Society', in Bernard McGinn, John Meyendorff and Jean Leclercq (eds), *Christian Spirituality 1: Origins to the Twelfth Century*, New York, 1986, pp.163–176.

CHAPTER TWO

1. Richard Morris, p.104.

2. Andrew Louth in *The Wilderness of God*, London, 1991, represents a recent attempt to describe the special qualities of the religion of the desert. The essay 'The Wilderness in the Medieval West' by Jacques Le Goff in his *The Medieval Imagination*, English translation, London/ Chicago, 1988, has some illuminating remarks on the understanding of 'desert' in western monasticism, including the Celtic tradition.

3. Alan O. Anderson and Marjorie O. Anderson (eds), *Adomnan's Life of Columba*, Oxford, 1991, pp.166–167.

4. Peter Harbison, *Pilgrimage in Ireland*, London, 1991, p.208.

5. See Bitel, *Isle of the Saints*, p.17. For a general survey of settlement sites see Bowen, Chapter VIII 'Settlements'.

6. Richard Morris, p.110.

7. Bowen, pp.204–206.

8. Lives cited respectively in Bitel, *Isle of the Saints*, pp.36–37 and Hughes and Hamlin, p.28.

9. See Bowen, pp.209–210.

10. Bede, *Ecclesiastical History*, ed. Colgrave and Mynors, Book IV, Chapter 25.

11. See Bitel, *Isle of the Saints*, pp.36–37.

12. Bede, Book iii, Chapter 23. See the translation by Leo Shirley-Price, edited with a new introduction and notes by D.H. Farmer, London, 1990, p.181.

13. Hughes and Hamlin, p.vii.

14. For a detailed description of the site, see Bowen, pp.196–200.

15. On ascetical motives for sites, see Richard Morris pp.113–114 and Hughes and Hamlin, pp.19–21.

16. Bowen, pp.191–195.

17. See Hughes and Hamlin, pp.22–27; Bitel, *Isle of the Saints*, pp.19–23.

18. See Chadwick, *The Celts*, p.213.

19. See Hughes and Hamlin, p.29.

20. See Bitel, *Isle of the Saints*, pp.39–56.

CHAPTER THREE

1. Cited in Richard Morris, p.104.

2. See Charles Thomas, p.149.

3. See, for example, Painton Cowan, *Rose Windows*, London, 1979.

4. See Bitel, *Isle of the Saints*, pp.58–60.

5. See Bitel, *Isle of the Saints*, p.82.

6. See Michael Maher (ed.), *Irish Spirituality*, Dublin, 1981, p.11; Bitel, *Isle of the Saints*, pp.1, 80–94; also Hughes and Hamlin, pp.6, 16.

7. I shall look specifically at the example of Iona in the Conclusion. For details of monastic life at the Abbey during the Middle Ages, see Alan Macquarrie and E. Mairi MacArthur, *Iona Through the Ages*, Society of West Highland & Island Historical Research, Isle of Coll, 2nd edition, 1992, pp.13–23.

8. See Bitel, *Isle of the Saints*, pp. 61–63.

9. Quoted in Maher (ed.), p.29. Original rule edited by E.J. Gwynn and W.J. Purtin, Section 6 of the *comrair chrabaid*.

10. See Hughes and Hamlin, pp.13–15, 54; also Hughes, *Church and Society*, Section 8 'The Church and the World in Early Christian Ireland', p.111.

11. See Hughes, *Church and Society*, p.111; also Riché, pp.169–170.

12. See Richard Morris, p.118; Hughes and Hamlin, p.73; and Hughes, *Church and Society*, Section 8, p.109.

13. Maire Herbert, *Iona, Kells and Derry: The History and Hagiography of the Monastic Familia of Columba*, Oxford, 1988, pp.105–106.

14. Kathleen Hughes, *Early Christian Ireland: Introduction to the Sources*, London, 1972, pp.267–268. On the twelfth-century changes,

see the *Annals of Ulster*, ed. B. MacCarthy, Dublin, 1893, Volume II, p.141.

15. Herbert, p.103.

16. See Bitel, *Isle of the Saints*, pp.126, 142–144; Hughes and Hamlin, pp.6–7; Hughes, *Early Christian Ireland*, pp.93–94; Hughes, *Church and Society*, Section 1, p.19, Section 8, p.109.

17. See Diarmuid O Laoghaire, 'Soul Friendship' in Lavinia Byrne (ed.), *Traditions of Spiritual Guidance*, London, 1990, p.30.

18. Cited in Hughes and Hamlin, p.7. On women and men in monastic enclosure, see also, Hughes and Hamlin, pp.7–9; McNeill, p.71; Lisa Bitel, 'Women's Monastic Enclosures in Early Ireland: A Study of Female Spirituality and Male Monastic Mentalities' in *Journal of Medieval History*, 12 (1986), pp.15–36. Bede's comments on Coldingham and Whitby appear in his *Ecclesiastical History*, Book iv, Sections 23–25.

19. On education, see Bede's *Ecclesiastical History*, Book III, Section 27; Hughes and Hamlin, pp.9–11, 75; McNeill, pp.73–74.

20. Bitel, *Isle of the Saints*, pp.201–202; Hughes and Hamlin, pp.14, 75.

21. On solitary life in relationship to religious settlements, see Bitel, *Isle of the Saints*, p.79; Hughes and Hamlin, pp.44, 74; Hughes, *Early Christian Ireland*, pp.92–93, 202–204. On the development of private penance, see Chadwick, *The Celts*, p.211.

CHAPTER FOUR

1. See Mark Redknapp, *The Christian Celts: Treasures of Late Celtic Wales*, Cardiff, 1991, pp.50–57.

2. See Royal Commission on the Ancient and Historical Monuments of Scotland. *Argyll: An Inventory of the Monuments. Volume 4. Iona.* Edinburgh, 1982, pp.17–19. Also Hughes and Hamlin, p.87.

3. See Malcolm Seaborne, *Celtic Crosses of Britain and Ireland*, Shire Archaeology Series. Aylesbury, 1989, p.8; Derek Bryce, *Symbolism of the Celtic Cross*, Lampeter, 1989, pp.11–13; Powell, *The Celts*, pp.1–65.

4. Seaborne, p.12.

6. See Richard Morris, p.84; Hughes and Hamlin, p.84; Hughes, *Early Christian Ireland*, pp.258–260.

7. See Seaborne, pp.5–6, 57; Hughes and Hamlin, p.96.

8. Cited in Hughes and Hamlin, p.80.

9. See Hughes and Hamlin, p.80; Bitel, *Isle of the Saints*, pp.64–66.

10. From a poem of about the ninth century in Gerard Murphy, *Early Irish Lyrics*, Oxford, 1956, no.9.

11. *Royal Commission*, pp.17–19; Seaborne, pp.5, 29–42.

12. See *Royal Commission*, p.18 and n.84; Seaborne, p.44; Hughes and Hamlin, p.90.

13. See Bryce, pp.33–40; Seaborne, pp.7–16; McNeill, p.128; Bulloch, p.118.

14. See Aidan Meehan, *Celtic Design: Spiral Patterns*, London, 1993, pp.46–47.

15. Meehan, pp.51–52.

16. See A.B.E. Hood (ed.), *St Patrick: His Writings and Muirchu's Life*, History from the Sources Series, Chichester, 1978, p.34 (and English translation p.53). There is an important recent article on St Patrick and the Christian unculturation of sun-worship – Timothy Powell, 'Christianity or Solar Monotheism: The Early Religious Beliefs of St Patrick' in *The Journal of Ecclesiastical History*, 43:4 (October 1992), pp.531–540.

17. See Bryce, pp.33–40.

18. John Anderson, 'The Voyage of Brendan, an Irish Monastic Expedition to Discover the Wonders of God's World', in *The American Benedictine Review*, 43:3 (September 1992), pp.273–274.

19. See McNeill, p.128; also Meehan, pp.23–54; Bradley, *The Celtic Way*, p.1.

20. Harbison, pp.122, 142.

21. See Jean Favier, *The World of Chartres*, London, English translation 1990, p.178. Also Cowan, p.85.

22. See J.A. MacCulloch, *The Religion of the Ancient Celts*, London, 1991 reprint, pp.340–341.

23. See Brown, *The Cult of the Saints*, pp.86–105. On relics and 'presence' at Iona and Kells, see Herbert, pp.80–81. See also Bitel, *Isle of the Saints*, p.57.

24. See Hughes and Hamlin, p.33.

25. See Hughes and Hamlin, p.107 and Charles Thomas, pp.136–139.

26. See Hughes and Hamlin, p.108 and Diarmuid O Laoghaire, 'Celtic Spirituality' in Jones, p.221.

CHAPTER FIVE

1. Bruce Chatwin, *Songlines*, London, 1988.

2. On this poem see, for example, the essay by Clair McPherson, 'The Sea a Desert: Early English Spirituality and *The Seafarer*', in *American Benedictine Review*, 38:2 (June 1987), pp.115–126.

3. For general surveys of the pilgrimage tradition, see Jonathan Sumption, *Pilgrimage, an Image of Medieval Religion*, London, 1975. On Celtic *peregrinatio* see Bowen, Chapter III 'The Saints and the Seaways'; and Harbison, especially Chapters 1–5. See also Chadwick, *The Celts*, p.204.

4. See Bowen, p.67.

5. Stanzas of a tenth-century Irish poem quoted in translation in Harbison, p.26.

6. *The Rule of St Benedict*, Chapter 1, 10–11, ed. Timothy Fry OSB, Collegeville, 1981.

7. Quoted in Mackey, p.155.

8. *Sancti Columbani Opera*, ed. G.S.M. Walker, Dublin, 1970, Sermon VIII, 2, p.97.

9. Quoted in Chadwick, *The Age of the Saints*, p.83.

10. Chadwick, *The Celts*, pp.280–282.

11. See MacCulloch, pp.344, 362, 369–71; also Riché, p.164; also Hughes and Hamlin, p.12.

12. See Cynthia Bourgeault, 'The Monastic Archetype in the *Navigatio* of St. Brendan' in *Monastic Studies*, 14 (Advent 1983), pp.109–121; also Anderson, pp.262–282.

13. See Hughes, *Early Christian Ireland*, p.212. Also Harbison, Chapter 5.

14. See Bowen, p.69.

15. Cited in Hughes, *Church and Society*, Section 9, pp.21–22.

16. See Bowen, pp.70–75.

17. See, for example, McNeill, p.155.

18. From the eleventh-century *The Voyage of the Ui Chorra*, quoted in Harbison, p.39.

19. See McNeill, pp.156–158; also Bitel, *Isle of the Saints*, p.223.

20. See O Laoghaire, 'Celtic Spirituality' in Jones, pp.219–220.

21. See Chadwick, *The Age of the Saints*, p.83. Also the Irish Life of Columba, cited in Herbert, pp.249–250.

22. See Chadwick, *The Age of the Saints*, pp.30–32. Also Harbison, pp.33–34.

23. *Sancti Columbani Opera*, Sermon VIII, 2; p.97, 11, 11–13.

24. See Hughes, *Church and Society in Ireland*, Section 14, p.143.

25. Cited in Chadwick, *The Age of the Saints*, pp.80–83.

26. See McNeill, pp.174–175; *Sancti Columbani Opera*, Letter IV. 4, p.29; Bede, *Ecclesiastical History*, trans. Shirley-Price, III, 19, p.172; Chadwick, *The Age of the Saints*, p.79.

27. *Adomnan's Life of Columba*, Anderson and Anderson (eds), i.6, pp.30–31.

28. Cited in Chadwick, *The Age of the Saints*, p.30. See also Bitel, *Isle of the Saints*, pp. 228–229.

29. On changing attitudes, see especially Kathleen Hughes, 'The Changing Theory and Practice of Irish Pilgrimage' in *The Journal of Ecclesiastical History* 11 (1960), pp.143–151.

30. *A Celtic Miscellany*, translated by Kenneth Hurlstone Jackson, London, 1971, no.224 'The Hermit', p.281.

31. Jackson, no.121, p.136.

32. Bitel, *Isle of the Saints*, pp.227–228.

33. A colleague, Dr David Cornick of Westminster College Cambridge, has suggested that our understanding of the 'usefulness' of the Celtic wanderers might benefit from an extension of Peter Brown's view of the holy man in late antiquity. Brown argues that an important feature of the holy man was to be removed from stable, conventional social structures. This very dysfunctionality gave holy men a powerful spiritual and social role. See Peter Brown, 'The Rise and Function of the Holy Man in Late Antiquity' in *Society and the Holy in Late Antiquity*, London, 1982, pp.103–152.

CHAPTER SIX

1. See, for example, Christopher Bamford and William Parker Marsh (eds), *Celtic Christianity: Ecology and Holiness*, New York, 1987.

2. For example, the old white horse who wept at the death of Columba of Iona in Adomnan's *Life*. See Anderson and Anderson (eds), pp.221–223.

3. For examples of monastic nature poetry see Jackson (ed.), nos 222–224. See also Alexander Carmichael, *Carmina Gadelica*, Edinburgh, 1992.

4. See Chadwick, *The Celts*, p.182.

5. See Hughes, *Church and Society*, Section 1, pp.12–13.

6. See *Adomnan's Life of Columba*, p.45.

7. For an interesting approach to medieval attitudes to nature, see A. Gurevitch, *Medieval Popular Culture: Problems of Belief and Perception*, Cambridge, 1990, pp.81–82, 95–97. I have relied a great deal on Gurevitch's insights in the paragraphs that follow.

8. See Chapter 3, pp.34–35.

9. See Hughes, *Early Christian Ireland*, pp.202–204.

10. See 'The Hermit's Song' in Patrick Murray (ed.), *The Deer's Cry:*

A Treasury of Irish Religious Verse, Dublin, 1986, pp.36–37. There is an alternative version in *A Celtic Miscellany*, p.280.

11. See Hughes and Hamlin, p.3.

12. See Hughes and Hamlin, p.4.

13. For all three quotations, see Sermon I, in Walker (ed.), *Sancti Columbani Opera*, pp.63, 65.

14. See preface to Carmichael, *Carmina Gadelica*, 1992. An extensive and excellent selection of prayers from the *Carmina Gadelica* have also been edited by Esther de Waal in *The Celtic Vision*, London, 1988. The full edition was published in six volumes (including a volume of notes) by the Scottish Academic Press, Edinburgh. References are to this edition, published as follows: Volume I reprinted 1984, Volume II reprinted 1984, Volume III reprinted 1976, Volume IV reprinted 1988, Volume V reprinted 1987, Volume VI reprinted 1988. Subsequent references are to this six-volume edition.

15. Jackson, no.222, p.279.

16. Jackson, no.234, p.296.

17. Robert Van de Weyer, *Celtic Fire*, London, 1990.

18. Full prayer in *Carmina Gadelica*, Volume I, pp.39–41 (extract).

19. Jackson, p.73.

20. *Carmina Gadelica*, Volume II, p.173 (extract).

21. *Carmina Gadelica*, Volume III, p.7 (extract).

22. *Carmina Gadelica*, Volume III, p.93 (extract).

23. *Carmina Gadelica*, Volume I, p.231 (extract).

24. *Carmina Gadelica*, Volume IV, p.65 (extract).

25. *Carmina Gadelica*, Volume I, p. 85 (extract).

26. For some rich comments on this closeness of the 'other world', see O'Donoghue, 'St Patrick's Breastplate' in Mackey (ed.), pp.50–53.

CONCLUSION

1. See Anderson and Anderson (eds), *Adomnan's Life of Columba*, p.233.

2. See John Patterson, *Iona: A Celebration*, London, 1987, p.19.

3. See Patterson, pp.8–9.

4. See Patterson, p.11.

5. MacCarthy (ed.), *Annals of Ulster*, Volume II, p.145.

6. Patterson, pp.23–24. Also Royal Commission on the Ancient and Historical Monuments of Scotland. *Argyll: An Inventory of the Monuments. Volume 4. Iona*, pp.34–36.

7. See Hughes, *Early Christian Ireland*, p.263 and Herbert, p.72.

8. See Herbert, p.72.

9. See Patterson, pp.9–10.

10. See Patterson, pp.9–10.

11. *Adomnan's Life*, p.225.

12. *The Irish Life of Adamnan*, ed. Maire Herbert and Padraig O Riain, Dublin, 1988, for example pp.253–254, 261.

13. The story is cited in Jackson, pp.296–297.

14. See Royal Commission, p.144.

15. *Adomnan's Life of Columba*, p.83.

16. See Royal Commission, pp.17–19.

17. See Royal Commission, p.250.

18. See Herbert, pp.28–29.

19. Cited in Herbert, pp.248, 260.

20. *Adomnan's Life of Columba*, pp.6–7.

21. *Adomnan's Life*, p. 217.

22. *Adomnan's Life*, pp.29–31.

23. See Chadwick, *The Celts*, p.182.

Works Cited

Alan O. Anderson and Marjorie O. Anderson (eds), *Adomnan's Life of Columba*, Oxford, 1991.

John Anderson, 'The Voyage of Brendan, an Irish Monastic Expedition to Discover the Wonders of God's World', in *The American Benedictine Review*, 43:3 (September 1992).

Christopher Bamford and William Parker Marsh (eds), *Celtic Christianity: Ecology and Holiness*, New York, 1987.

M.W. Barley and R.P.C. Hanson (eds), *Christianity in Britain 300–700*, Leicester, 1968.

Bede, *Ecclesiastical History of the English People*, ed. B. Colgrave, and R.A.B. Mynors, Oxford, 1969.

Bede, *Ecclesiastical History of the English People*, trans. Leo Shirley-Price, London, 1990.

Lisa Bitel, *Isle of the Saints: Monastic Settlement and Christian Community in Early Ireland*, Ithaca, New York, 1990.

Lisa Bitel, 'Women's Monastic Enclosures in Early Ireland: A Study of Female Spirituality and Male Monastic Mentalities' in *Journal of Medieval History*, 12 (1986).

Cynthia Bourgeault, 'The Monastic Archetype in the *Navigatio* of St Brendan', in *Monastic Studies*, 14, (Advent 1983).

E.G. Bowen, *Saints, Seaways and Settlements*, Cardiff, 1977.

Ian Bradley, *The Celtic Way*, London, 1993,

Peter Brown, *The Cult of the Saints*, London, 1981.

Peter Brown, *Society and the Holy in Late Antiquity*, London, 1982.

Derek Bryce, *Symbolism of the Celtic Cross*, Lampeter, 1989.

James Bulloch, *The Life of the Celtic Church*, Edinburgh, 1963.

Alexander Carmichael, *Carmina Gadelica*, Single Volume Edition, Edinburgh, 1992.

Alexander Carmichael, *Carmina Gadelica*, Six Volume Edition, Edinburgh, Vol.1 reprinted 1983; Vol.2 reprinted 1972; Vol.3 1940; Vol.4 1941; Vol.5 1954; Vol. 6 Notes.

Nora Chadwick, *The Age of the Saints in the Early Celtic Church*, London, 1961.

Nora Chadwick, *The Celts*, London, 1971.

Bruce Chatwin, *Songlines*, London, 1988.

Painton Cowan, *Rose Windows*, London, 1979.

Esther de Waal, *A World Made Whole*, London, 1991

Esther de Waal, *The Celtic Vision*, London, 1988.

J.A. Duke, *The Columban Church*, Edinburgh, 1957.

Jean Favier, *The World of Chartres*, London, 1990.

W.H. Frend, 'Ecclesia Britannica: Prelude or Dead End?' in *The Journal of Ecclesiastical History*, 30:2 (April 1979).

Valerie Flint, *The Rise of Magic in Early Medieval Europe*, Oxford, 1991.

Timothy Fry (ed.), *The Rule of St Benedict*, Collegeville, 1981.

A. Gurevitch, *Medieval Popular Culture: Problems of Belief and Perception*, Cambridge, 1990.

Peter Harbison, *Pilgrimage in Ireland*, London, 1991.

Maire Herbert, *Iona, Kells and Derry: The History and Hagiography of the Monastic Familia of Columba*, Oxford, 1988.

Maire Herbert and Padraig O Riain (eds), *The Irish Life of Adamnan*, Dublin, 1988.

A.B.E. Hood (ed.), *St Patrick: His Writings and Muirchu's Life*, Chichester, 1978.

Kathleen Hughes, *Church and Society in Ireland AD 400–1200*, London, 1987.

Kathleen Hughes, *Early Christian Ireland: Introduction to the Sources*, London, 1972.

Kathleen Hughes, 'The Changing Theory and Practice of Irish Pilgrimage', in *The Journal of Ecclesiastical History*, 11 (1960).

Kathleen Hughes and Ann Hamlin, *Celtic Monasticism: The Modern Traveller to the Irish Church*, New York, 1981.

Kenneth Hurlstone Jackson (ed.), *A Celtic Miscellany*, London, 1971.

Jacques Le Goff, *The Medieval Imagination*, London/Chicago, 1988.

Andrew Louth, *The Wilderness of God*, London, 1991.

B. MacCarthy (ed.), *Annals of Ulster*, Dublin, 1893.

Alan Macquarrie and E. Mairi MacArthur, *Iona Through the Ages*, Isle of Coll, 1991.

J.A. MacCulloch, *The Religion of the Ancient Celts*, London, 1991.

John T. McNeill, *The Celtic Churches: A History AD 200–1200*, Chicago, 1974.

Clair McPherson, 'The Sea a Desert: Early English Spirituality and *The Seafarer*', in *The American Benedictine Review*, 38:2 (June 1987).

James Mackey (ed.), *An Introduction to Celtic Christianity*, Edinburgh, 1989.

Michael Maher (ed.), *Irish Spirituality*, Dublin, 1981.

Aidan Meehan, *Celtic Design: Spiral Patterns*, London, 1993.

Richard Morris, *Churches in the Landscape*, London, 1989.

Gerard Murphy (ed.), *Early Irish Lyrics*, Oxford, 1956.

Patrick Murray (ed.), *The Deer's Cry: A Treasury of Irish Religious Verse*, Dublin, 1986.

Diarmuid O Laoghaire, 'Celtic Spirituality' in Cheslyn Jones, Geoffrey Wainwright and Edward Yarnold (eds), *The Study of Spirituality*, London, 1986.

Diarmuid O Laoghaire, 'Soul Friendship' in Lavinia Byrne (ed.), *Traditions of Spiritual Guidance*, London/Collegeville, 1990.

John Patterson, *Iona: A Celebration*, London, 1987.

T.G.E. Powell, *The Celts*, London, 1980.

T.G.E. Powell, 'Christianity or Solar Monotheism: The Early Religious Beliefs of St Patrick' in *The Journal of Ecclesiastical History*, 43:4 (October 1992).

Mark Redknapp, *The Christian Celts: Treasures of Late Celtic Wales*, Cardiff, 1991.

Alwyn and Brinley Rees, *Celtic Heritage: Ancient Tradition in Ireland and Wales*, London, reprint 1990.

Pierre Riché, 'Spirituality in Germanic and Celtic Society', in Bernard McGinn, etc. (eds), *Christian Spirituality 1: Origins to the Twelfth Century*, New York, 1986.

Royal Commission on the Ancient and Historical Monuments of Scotland, *Argyll: An Inventory of the Monuments. Volume 4 Iona*, Edinburgh, 1982.

Malcolm Seaborne, *Celtic Crosses of Britain and Ireland*, Aylesbury, 1989.

Richard Sharpe, 'Churches and Communities in Early Medieval Ireland: Towards a Pastoral Model', in John Blair and Richard Sharpe (eds), *Pastoral Care Before the Parish*, Leicester, 1992.

Philip Sheldrake, *Spirituality and History: Questions of Interpretation and Method*, London/New York, 1992.

Jonathan Sumption, *Pilgrimage: An Image of Medieval Religion*, London, 1975.

Charles Thomas, *Celtic Britain*, London, 1986.

Patrick Thomas, *Candle in the Darkness: Celtic Spirituality from Wales*, Llandysul, Dyfed, 1993.

G.S.M. Walker (ed.), *Sancti Columbani Opera*, Dublin, 1970.

Anton Wessels, *Europe: Was It Ever Really Christian?*, London, 1994.

Patrick Wormald, 'The Venerable Bede and the "Church of the English" ', in Geoffrey Rowell (ed.), *The English Religious Tradition and the Genius of Anglicanism*, Wantage, 1993.

Index